# THROUGH MIRACLES TO MINISTRY

# THROUGH MIRACLES TO MINISTRY

ERICKSON FABIEN

Copyright © 2014 by Erickson Fabien.

Library of Congress Control Number:     2014916024
ISBN:        Hardcover        978-1-4990-2022-9
             Softcover        978-1-4990-2024-3
             eBook            978-1-4990-2026-7

All rights reserved. No part of this book may be reproduced or transmitted in any form or by any means, electronic or mechanical, including photocopying, recording, or by any information storage and retrieval system, without permission in writing from the copyright owner.

Any people depicted in stock imagery provided by Thinkstock are models, and such images are being used for illustrative purposes only.
Certain stock imagery © Thinkstock.

Rev. date: 11/17/2014

To order additional copies of this book, contact:
Xlibris
1-800-455-039
www.Xlibris.com.au
Orders@Xlibris.com.au

# CONTENTS

Dedication ............................................................................................. 7
Acknowledgments ................................................................................ 9

I—God's Miraculous Call .................................................................. 11
II—My Samuel Years: 1973-2001 ..................................................... 17
III—The Turning Point ...................................................................... 39
IV—Forward In Faith ......................................................................... 50
V—Journey of Blessings .................................................................... 59
VI—The Philippine Experience ......................................................... 74
VII—In the Field ................................................................................ 86
VIII—Epilogue ................................................................................... 97

## Dedication

This book is dedicated to

…my dear wife Jacqueline, and my two lovely children, Annique and Christopher, who have taken the last 18-21 years of this incredible journey with me.

…the memory of the late Dr. Kenneth D. Mulzac, a man of God who touched countless lives;

…my lifelong friend, Sheryl White, to whom I promised to dedicate my first book.

## Acknowledgments

Unless otherwise stated, all scripture references are from the New King James Version. Copyright © 1982 by Thomas Nelson, Inc. Used by permission. All rights reserved.

Scripture credited to NIV is taken from the HOLY BIBLE, NEW INTERNATIONAL VERSION®. Copyright © 1973, 1978, 1984 Biblica. Used by permission of Zondervan. All rights reserved.

Scripture credited to GW is taken from GOD'S WORD®, © 1995 God's Word to the Nations. Used by permission of Baker Publishing Group.

Thanks to:

…Gerry Bird for permission to reprint his photo of the Bequia Seventh-day Adventist Secondary School;

…Belynda McClendon Mulzac for permission to reprint the Mulzac family photo;

… Figuhr Fabien and Rosita Lashley for proofreading my manuscript.

# 1

# GOD'S MIRACULOUS CALL

> *The word of the Lord came to me, saying, "Before I formed you in the womb I knew you, before you were born I set you apart; I appointed you as a prophet to the nations."*
>
> *"Alas, Sovereign Lord," I said, "I do not know how to speak; I am too young."*
>
> *But the Lord said to me, "Do not say, 'I am too young.' You must go to everyone I send you to and say whatever I command you. Do not be afraid of them, for I am with you and will rescue you," declares the Lord. Jeremiah 1:4-7, NIV.*

## *Prologue*

Nineteen ninety-one.

The year America invaded Iraq under the code name Operation Desert Storm.

The year the Soviet Union crumbled.

The year after the year Nelson Mandela walked free, ending twenty-seven years in prison.

Nineteen ninety-one: my final undergraduate year at Caribbean Union College in Trinidad.

I'm lying on my bunk bed early one spring morning, drowsy but wide awake. A familiar knock and shout echoes down the dormitory halls. It's more of a bang than a knock, actually. The knocker-banger-shouter is using some hard object, possibly a scrubbing brush, going from door to do, rousing the slumbering down from their wooden bunks, summoning them to morning worship.

"Let's make it, boys! Let's go! Come out! Come down! It's worship time!"

The banging and shouting gets louder... louder, closer! I lie there, wishing... hoping he would pass my door. Why? Because he doesn't need to bang and shout. My roommate Lester and I are always at morning worship. Always! We often play the piano or lead the singing, and he knows that. He's the dean, and in a small dormitory like ours, the dean knows everybody.

Well, so much for wishing. He bangs.

But this morning, something different happens. He doesn't shout!

Peter—for that was his name—doesn't shout. He simply OPENS the door and walks right in. He has never done this before. Never! The next thing I know is that he's standing inside near the little table which is to the left of the door and calling to me.

"Fabien, what are you studying?"

"Social Studies major with Secondary Teacher Training," I answer.

"Really? You know, I always thought you were studying theology. Man, are you sure you're in the right program?"

My mind races. Where have I heard this before? Sounds familiar and funny.

"Well," I reply, half chuckling, "theology is for guys preparing for pastoral ministry, and for that, you must be called by God. I'm sure I haven't been called."

"Well," countered Peter, "I think…(pause)… you should seriously think about taking theology. I believe you have what it takes. I know you're in your final year but it's not too late."

Back home, we use the French creole expression, *"Oui c'est la paix"* (pronounced wee say lah pay). It means that saying "Yes" brings peace; it ends the argument, in other words. So I say, "Ok, Dean. I'll think about it."

And sure enough, Peter turns around, walks out, and continues banging and shouting at other doors.

That was nineteen ninety-one, a year I will never forget.

## *Simon and the Saviour's Call*

But let's leave 1991. Let's travel back in time.

Come with me. Let's journey back to first-century Palestine, to a region known as Galilee. Our destination? A lake. A lake so huge that it's commonly called a sea. Come with me to the Sea of Galilee.

We're in the past; remember? So there are no buses or cabs to get around here; only horses, mules or donkeys. And, of course, a steady pair of legs and strong sandals for your feet: you're going to need those.

We're making an early start from our little bread-n-breakfast inn (which doesn't even have a star rating). We want to get there before the morning heats up too much. What's more, something amazing is about to happen down at the water's edge and we don't want to miss it.

Through a series of twists and turns, climbing over rocky outcrops and stepping carefully onto loosened boulders, brushing our legs against resilient scrubland bushes on either side of the trail, we negotiate our way downhill, occasionally pausing for a few seconds to catch the breath-taking view—the distant western hills bathed in glorious morning sunlight and the shimmering waters of Lake Galilee hundreds of feet below. Soon, the steep descent gives way to gentler lowland and

## THROUGH MIRACLES TO MINISTRY

we see the last few turns ahead. Our excitement grows. Our anticipation heightens. Our footsteps quicken.

Taddah! Here we are.

We've made it. It sure feels good to be here. Up there on those slopes it was getting a bit chilly, but down here it's significantly warmer, thanks to a balmy breeze blowing our way. We rip off our dusty sandals and tiptoe gingerly over a few meters of rounded pebbles to where the ripples are gently breaking. The water! Ah! Now THAT feels good! We wish we could stay right there. But that's not why we came. Remember? Something amazing is about to happen and we don't want to miss it.

Actually, there's quite a lot happening around us, but more than anything else, we're interested in a particular group of men. Fishermen they are. They've just come ashore and they're still around their boat, sorting through the jumbled mass of their nets and picking out their exceedingly meagre catch from among the weeds and algae trapped therein.

As we walk toward them, we notice a little group farther up the shore. They're moving in our direction. Ahead of them walks someone stranger than anyone we've seen all morning. He is quite tall but ordinary looking and appears to be wearing a seamless robe fastened about His waist with a cord. His feet are shod with a pair of common sandals. His hair blows slightly in the morning breeze. His eyes seem to keenly survey the scene, noting the varied activities of fishing crews; yet, like us, He bypasses them with nothing but a friendly greeting. Like us, He's homing in on that one boat up ahead.

Soon, we are at equal distance from it and we're just in time to catch the starting point of a conversation between the Stranger and the fishermen.

"Hey, Simon. Can I stand in your boat for a while to talk to these people? I just need some space."

"No problem, Master," Simon accedes. Come on in."

Master?

Hm! Simon, whose surname quite uncannily turns out to be Peter, obviously knows this man quite well. He must be a famous teacher. Some guru! Somebody ... special!

While we're standing there trying to figure it out, the Stranger climbs aboard. Despite the boat's constant rocking, He maintains His balance with consummate ease and proceeds to address the curious crowd, sharing with them precious words of wisdom. But it's not just the wisdom of His words that grips us; it's the authority with which He says what He's saying. It's like... stuff that you've never heard before with an authority that you've never known before. Got it?

When He is done, He steps out of the boat, wades through the water toward the shore, turns around, looks Simon straight in the eye, and with a jerk of the head calmly says to Him,

"Let down your net, Simon, and take up some fish."

There's a pause. A look: a questioning, very sceptical kind of look. If Simon Peter wore glasses, he would be looking over the rim with deeply furrowed brows, first at the Stranger, then at those on his left and right whom he thinks might have heard what he thinks he has just heard.

13

"Let down my net! Master, are you…?" Simon respectfully aborts the rest of his sentence. "What are you saying?" he half exclaims, half questions. "We've been toiling literally all night out here, while you were… er… asleep! Yea, asleep; and look! Zilch! Zero! Nothing! And now, you…"

Simon stops mid-sentence. The look on that Stranger's face says it all: "Simon, this is not up for discussion. Why don't you just do what I told you?"

"Ok. Ok, Master," he unwillingly concedes. "Since you say so, I'll do it. I'll do it. I will…er... just... er… let down my net… and… er… Yeah, I'll do it. I'll do it! Here we go!"

And with some help from his mates, Simon lets down the net.

"That's it, Master. Net's down—just as the Master ordered!"

What happens next should be easy to describe and dramatize, but I'll let the Bible speak. Luke, the beloved physician-historian, puts it this way: "And when they had done this, they caught a great number of fish, and their net was breaking. So they signalled to their partners in the other boat to come and help them. And they came and filled both the boats, so that they began to sink" (Luke 5:6, 7).

What a jaw dropper! What an amazing manifestation of the power of God! What a stirring testament to the timeless promise, "God will provide!"

Simon Peter is understandably shocked, but the expression on his face is not simply one of astonishment; he is equally delighted! Never in his fishing career, yea, in his entire life, has he witnessed anything of this sort and on this scale. All at once, he finds himself staring at a potentially massive financial windfall. In today's parlance, Simon has hit the jackpot! He's on cloud nine!

But something else is stirring inside him. Simon Peter recognizes that he has just been blessed in a manner and measure that he does not deserve. He suddenly sees himself as a vile, good-for-nothing, repeat offender, someone whose smudgy character stands in stark contrast to that of his faultless and benevolent Master. And in a moment of utter self-abhorrence he throws himself at Jesus's knees and exclaims, "Depart from me, for I am a sinful man, O Lord!"

Luke concludes this pericope with the words, "And Jesus said to Simon, "Do not be afraid. From now on you will catch men." So when they had brought their boats to land, they forsook all and followed Him" (verses 10-11).

End of the story—at least for now! Thanks for taking the journey with me. It's been worth the trouble, hasn't it? I'm glad we made it in time to see the action, because what we've just witnessed will help me make a crucial point and thus set the stage for the longer story that I'm about to tell you.

## *Preliminary Point to Ponder*

I don't know which part of that narrative caught your attention, but I particularly love the way it ended—with the divine call, the call to go fish for people. That, my dear friends, is what grabs me. That is what drives me. That is what has moved me to write—because it is something with which I can identify.

## THROUGH MIRACLES TO MINISTRY

Now I've spent a lot of time thinking about this call and I've come up with seven observations in its regard, six of which I will share at the very end of this book. But here's the first one:

*God's call often comes in the context of miracles.*

Stop for a while. Think about it. Let your mind go back to the Sea of Galilee. Can you see it?

Here's a miraculous catch of fish... and the next thing we hear is what? The call! The call to go fishing for people.

Voila!

I can take you on a whirlwind tour of the Bible. There, we'll encounter Moses and the miracle of the burning bush; we'll see his leprous hand and watch his rod turn to a serpent and back again to a rod. We'll find Gideon with the miracle of wet fleece on dry ground and the dry fleece on wet ground. We'll find King Saul miraculously prophesying under the power of God's Spirit. We'll also find Isaiah whose unclean lips are supernaturally transformed by the touch of a live coal from the altar. We'll find Jeremiah also being touched by the hand of Jehovah. And we'll find Saul of Tarsus being struck with blindness on the Damascus Road, only to be miraculously healed and commissioned three days later.

So there are numerous examples of call being tagged to at least one miracle. And why?

And why not? After all, it does take some doing to convince someone who sees himself as "the least of the least" that God is actually planning to use him to accomplish something special.

Miracles are amazing things! They have the power to dispel doubt, answer questions, and quell arguments. They have the power to convince. John, the beloved disciple, wrote his entire gospel account out of this recognition. He stated in chapter 20, verses 30 through 32, that "Jesus performed many other miracles that his disciples saw. Those miracles are not written in this book. But these miracles have been written so that you will believe that Jesus is the Messiah, the Son of God, and so that you will have life by believing in him" (GW).

Here's a classic case of God responding to human doubt by performing a miracle. According to Luke's gospel, Zechariah the priest was ministering beside the sacred altar in Jerusalem one day when he had an angelic visit. The heavenly messenger informed him that his wife Elizabeth would have a son who would go in the spirit and power of Elijah to prepare the way of the Lord. That in itself would have to be a miracle, for in Zechariah's own words, he was an old man and his wife had passed her child-bearing years (see Luke 1:18). Naturally, the old man asked for proof. Wouldn't you?

"The angel replied, 'I'm Gabriel! I stand in God's presence. God sent me to tell you this good news. But because you didn't believe what I said, you will be unable to talk until the day this happens'" (Luke 1:19-20, GW).

This was no pleasant sign. Good old Zech was struck with sudden dumbness and, much to the consternation of his family and friends, remained unable to speak until the birth of his miracle boy. It's as if God had said to him, "You want proof? Well, how's that for incontrovertible proof?"

Hang on. Pause for a moment. I don't want you walking away from this chapter thinking, "Hey, if there was no miracle, that wasn't a divine call." Let's get this clear: God doesn't get stuck in a rut the way we humans are prone to do. God has an innumerable variety of mysterious and unpredictable ways to get the job done—and He uses them at will. Sometimes, He calls by means of dreams and visions. Sometimes, His voice is heard through significant events in people's lives. At other times, He speaks through keen, discerning members of the household of faith: a pastor, an elder, a youth leader, or just some faithful old brother or sister in the congregation, or some dormitory dean named Peter paying an odd early morning visit. That's just the way God is; that's how He operates.

In Bible times, He didn't always call from out of a burning bush, did He? Nor did He always send a prophet. God even used an open election process to choose Matthias as a replacement for Judas among the 120 apostles (see Acts 1:15-26). So please keep that in mind.

As I trace God's leading in my life and reflect on His call to the pastoral ministry, I can see a long string of miracles. I haven't always recognized them, but it appears that their frequency and timeliness seemed to increase from the moment I recognized and chose to follow the call. Looking back, I can create some sort of a chronology of those miracles, but in this book, I will only mention a few which occurred prior to my acceptance of God's call; the remainder will focus on how God led afterward.

Having said all of that, I want to sit at your confession box for a while. I want to admit that I am still utterly amazed that God would ever call someone like me to do anything for Him. I've often felt like borrowing the lines from an old ring game we used to play as kids ("Who Stole the Cookie?") to describe the conversation going on between me and God. It's like,

"Who? Me?" I would ask.

"Yes, you!" God would reply.

Couldn't be!" I'd protest.

"Then who?" God would ask, not that He wanted me to suggest someone else; rather, He was in fact stating that I was the best man for the job.

No! Really... seriously, I've never felt I deserved to be called. I guess it's just the way I see myself—the result of that searching inward look. I don't like what I see, so I'm left wondering what God sees in me. But hey! When I gaze upward... (Hallelujah!), I sense God's amazing grace and mercy as I'm led to acknowledge that it's not **because of** me but **in spite of** me that He called.

Let me declare, finally, that my ultimate purpose for sharing all that appears hereafter is simply and exclusively to encourage someone out there to trust God, thereby giving Him glory. I dare not take one iota of credit or one strand of praise for the outcome of any of the events mentioned in this book. Rather, I boast of the goodness of God, the faithfulness of His word, and the reliability of His promises. I wish to exalt the value of prayer and the virtue of simple childlike faith. I believe that my testimony of God's dealings can serve to strengthen the faith of anyone who reads it. After all, if God did it for me, He can do it for anyone.

Hey! Let's make that personal: He can do it for YOU!

## II

# MY SAMUEL YEARS: 1973-2001

> *Then the Lord called yet again, "Samuel!"*
> *So Samuel arose and went to Eli, and said, "Here I am, for you called me." He answered, "I did not call, my son; lie down again." (Now Samuel did not yet know the Lord, nor was the word of the Lord yet revealed to him.) And the Lord called Samuel again the third time. So he arose and went to Eli, and said, "Here I am, for you did call me." Then Eli perceived that the Lord had called the boy. Therefore Eli said to Samuel, "Go, lie down; and it shall be, if He calls you, that you must say, 'Speak, Lord, for Your servant hears.'" So Samuel went and lay down in his place 1 Samuel 3:6-9.*

### *Prologue*

Stick with me because we're about to embark on another journey. We're following a long and winding trail which starts in my home village of Bense, a small agricultural community located on the northeast coast of a rugged but naturally beautiful Eastern Caribbean island known as Dominica. Let's go.

It's about nine on a bright, sunny Saturday morning around April of 1973. You're trudging up the dirt and gravel roads of Bense, and on your way, you pass scores of well-dressed, book-bearing villagers, young and old, heading in the opposite direction: they are on their way to church.

Among them are five siblings, three girls and two boys, with their parents: a six-foot, bald, slightly bow-legged man with his much shorter, pleasingly plump, smooth-skinned, hat-wearing wife. Although they walk together as a family, the children are intentionally a few paces ahead, remaining under the ever-watchful eyes of their parents.

You continue on your journey, but at about four thirty in the afternoon, as you're trekking back down the hills to the main road, your curiosity gets the better of you, so you stop by the church and peep through the aluminium-louvered windows to get a glimpse of the goings-on inside.

Up front are a few youngsters excitedly playing some sort of game. One of them, a rather skinny chap wearing a little puffy afro, a pair of blue trousers and a perpetual grin, catches your attention. He seems to be scoring lots of points for his team. And then it all comes back: he was one of those five siblings walking down the hill with their bald-headed father and pleasingly plump mother earlier that day. That was him.

Yes, that was me.

Bense Seventh-day Adventist Church

## *Budding at Bense*

I grew up in a church-going family. We attended church religiously (of course! How else?) every Saturday, both morning and afternoon. But we didn't just attend church; we were active participants in the services and activities. And that was on account of who my parents were.

You see, my father, Mederick (pronounced a bit like Frederick), was for many years the leading elder of our congregation. In that role, he preached countless sermons in his unique teaching style, performed numerous child dedications, conducted a few funerals, visited many members, chaired regular church board and other committee meetings, and even mediated occasional disputes among people in the community. Daddy, as we siblings all called him, took his church leadership role seriously... very seriously—so seriously, in fact, that he earned himself the nickname of Pope. It was a nickname which I suspect he resented at first but later took with a pinch of humour. But he was a stickler for discipline and order, and when he thought it necessary to maintain that order, he would not hesitate to take a firm, fearless stand.

Daddy was also an active church planter. He spent many hours on the road, travelling to communities around the island with other members of the Adventist Laymen's Federation, helping to raise and strengthen several new congregations including one in the Carib Territory, home to the island's surviving indigenous people, the Caribs. In those days, transportation was scarce so he often walked. I retain indelible memories of him arriving home after being absent for a day and a half on one of those "mission trips." Up those front steps he came, and we, happy to have him back, would invariably move toward him; as we did, he would bend over and kiss each of us in turn. I remember feeling his unshaven beard pricking my tender face as the distinct smell of motor vehicle fumes on his clothes told the tale of a man who had spent at least an hour sitting at the back of some open truck.

My dad in more recent times

My deceased mother, Josephine, was a church leader in her own right. She often led the Sabbath School, our version of Sunday School, as well as the Deaconess ministry and the Dorcas Society, the community services arm of our church. She was also quite involved in leading the singing at corporate worship. But more than that, she stood solidly behind my father so he could carry on the active lifestyle that his church leadership and church planting demanded. Mama bore days and nights of taking care of the young family while Daddy was on the road. When the laymen came over for their island-wide meetings, or when the pastors came a-calling, she played the crucial role of hostess. Sister Jojo, as she was also commonly known, was the good praying woman that people say stands behind every good man.

So knowingly or unwittingly, both my parents modelled church ministry.

That, my friends, had a profound effect on my life even if I did not realize what was happening. It literally shaped me. It was all I knew. I didn't know what it meant to go to church and just sit like a spectator, week after week; I was always involved. Sometimes it was because I was asked, sometimes because I volunteered, and sometimes because my family simply wanted to do something special at church. And when we were asked, my parents made sure that we practised and did it well. Quite often we made our presentations during the morning sessions; however, the afternoon programs, then called MV Meetings (MV meant Missionary Volunteer), gave us youngsters a lot of scope for using our budding talents and gifts in church ministry. MV was our training ground. We sang, recited, acted, competed, played, prayed, and even preached.

## *Blessings from Bourne*

But we had another training ground of which I dare not fail to speak; that was the Bourne Seventh-day Adventist Primary School. Housed in the Adventist Church in the tiny hilltop village of Bourne some five miles from home, the school brought together scores of children from its immediate vicinity as well as from the neighbouring communities of Portsmouth, Dos d'ane (pronounced doe-dann) and Bense.

At Bourne we sat at the feet of Christian teachers who not only instructed us in Reading, Writing and Arithmetic but also schooled us in the things of God. At Bourne we had our daily dose of devotions and Bible tuition as well as our own weekly MV Society meetings. Just like we did at church on Saturday afternoons, we learned to use our budding talents in various forms of church ministry.

I can just look back now and see little groups of students huddled together, planning what they were going to do for the next meeting. I can see a newly elected leadership team on the platform, having taken the helm at the start of the new school year. I can hear the notes of singing, the ripple of laughter, and the exclamations of rejoicing when one team won the Bible game. I can feel the cool hilltop wind blowing against our backs as we stood outside in a little prayer circle during the regularly-scheduled weeks of prayer. Yes, the Bourne School was for many good reasons the place to be, the place where one could be primed for ministry.

And do you know what? Attending the Bourne School was everything but convenient. In an age when transportation was truly scarce, travelling five Dominican miles to attend school when there was a public school just down the village road was sort of unreasonable, even crazy. But my parents, along with several others from our church community, decided to make the faith sacrifice so that their kids could obtain an Adventist education. (Hey! I am so thankful they did!)

On most days, we were taken to and from school by a dedicated, kind-hearted, now-deceased lay businessman from Portsmouth named Arthur Waldron, whom almost everybody I knew called Brother Waldron. But sometimes, especially on afternoons, Brother Waldron could not make it because of unforeseen circumstances, and whenever he couldn't come, we had to walk home! Yes, walk—five, miles of narrow, winding, tiring Dominican road, fraught with many dangers, not least of which were trucks speeding back to the countryside on their way from the Portsmouth harbour on banana harvesting days. I praise God that as far as I can recall, not one of us ever got seriously hurt on the journey home. He must have given His angels solemn charge over us to keep us in all our ways during those years.

It was on one of those afternoon treks from Bourne that I witnessed my first of many miracles. That day, the weather was everything but predictable. A bright and sunny hour could be easily and swiftly followed by a heavy tropical thunderstorm. Our little group of about twenty-five students knew the risk we were taking that afternoon. On the one hand, we dreaded the prospect of arriving home soaked to the bone, but on the other hand we had no choice: Brother Waldron had not come; so we simply had to press on and hope for the best.

Well, what do you suppose? We were just about halfway home when saw a huge white sheet of rain sweeping down the distant hills, heading straight for us. Like the Israelites at the Red Sea, we were cornered. There was literally nowhere to run, no place to seek shelter. A good soaking, schoolbooks and all, was just a matter of moments away.

Suddenly, one of the older students called out, "Everybody come! Come over here. Let's pray."

Like a brood of chickens responding to their mother-hen's call, we all rushed in that student's direction and huddled together as the first drops began to splatter on the asphalt road. Nobody stopped to question the wisdom of such a move; no one dared to argue. This was a case of bedtime-story faith springing alive. The student who had called prayed a short and very specific prayer, asking God to protect us from the rain.

Amen!

I opened my eyes. The scene before me was nothing short of a magnificent manifestation of the mercy, power, love and care of Almighty God. The rain, dear reader, was pelting down all around us, at least fifty metres on every side, but not a single drop was falling where we were standing! Not a single drop! It's as though we were standing under some huge invisible umbrella! Awesome indeed was the scene. And the next minute, just as swiftly as it had arrived, the deluge moved mysteriously on, blown over by a powerful blast of wind. God had proven His power to us that day as we put our trust in Him.

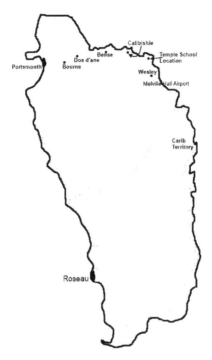

Sketch map of Dominica

## *Preacher in Preparation*

But let's return to my formative experiences at Bense church.

There are some things in life that you simply don't forget, and for me, it was the event I've just described as well as the one I'm about to relate, namely, my very first experience preaching a full-length sermon.

I was still just twelve years old and nowhere near my present height when I stood for the first time behind the huge, imposing, now-discarded wooden pulpit of my home church to preach. Correction: it wasn't "my" sermon, really; it was one of those "pre-cooked and canned" messages that came in the mail from the Youth Department at our regional headquarters in Barbados. The occasion was our annual Pathfinders' Day celebration; as such, it was not unusual to see a young speaker replace one of the older heads in the pulpit.

So there I was, not quite "trembling and astonished" like Saul on the Damascus Road (Acts 9:6) but still sufficiently awed by the occasion to work up a great deal of sweat. I was sitting there at first, anxiously watching everything else happening like undercard bouts before the main boxing event.

Before I knew it, the biggest moment of my life (up to that point) had arrived! I stood up to preach!

But I had a problem: I was too short. Yeah; laugh if you want. I was too short. Had I stood up at my natural height, the saints would only have been able to discern the top of my head. My youth leader, recognizing this, had therefore arranged to stack two wooden crates, which were normally used for storing bottled soft-drinks, right in front of me. I simply had to climb onto them. Therefore, when I stood up, I literally stood up.

After half reading and half reciting for a few minutes the script that I had reviewed quite extensively, I felt more confident and relaxed so I started trying to imitate the intonations and gestures that real preachers used in those days—at least as much as my still-boyish vocal tones and skinny frame would allow. Unfortunately, I couldn't move around like those preachers did, else I would have fallen off my perch. I did occasionally lose track of my exact location in the script but the saints were forgiving—as saints should be; they all said "Amen."

Perhaps the weirdest part of this whole episode was the way I concluded. It was more like an announcement than a conclusion. I simply said, "And this is the end of my sermon." Again, the brethren graciously said "Amen" but after having a few days to reflect on that conclusion, I couldn't help feeling that this rookie preacher had flunked his first test. That, by the way, was the last time ever that I ended a sermon in this fashion, for my very clever second-eldest sister made it her business for many days thereafter to poke some good-natured fun at me by repeating that line. And I got the message: THAT is NOT how you end a sermon!

Yet, the church leaders kept faith in me and I guess I kept growing in my ability to share an occasional message from the front desk. Thus it happened that by the time I was about eighteen going on nineteen, my church leaders asked me for the first time to preach an entire evangelistic series at our church. I thought I could do it, so I accepted.

The young preacher, around 1975

## *Fledgling Fisherman*

The decision to preach in this series was quite a significant one. It was a rather crazy one too. (Faith does seemingly crazy things! Don't you ever forget that!) You see, at that point in my life, I was attending the Sixth Form College in Roseau, the capital, preparing to write the University of Cambridge (England) General Certificate of Education Advanced Level Examinations. But—and here's the crazy part—I took four weeks away from school so that I could preach.

Yes, I dropped out of school to go preach!

For four long weeks!

Do you know how much can be lost by being absent from school for four consecutive weeks? Quite frankly, I knew the risk I was taking, but I reasoned that if I took those four weeks off to do God's work, He could do more than help me to pass my examinations. What's more, I had the support of my parents and an entire church community. And even if I didn't pass, I would be satisfied that I had done God's will. After all, what could be more important? In fact, I made Paul's declaration in Philippians 3:7-8 mine: "But whatever was to my profit I now consider loss for the sake of Christ. What is more, I consider everything a loss compared to the surpassing greatness of knowing Christ Jesus my Lord, for whose sake I have lost all things. I consider them rubbish that I may gain Christ" (NIV).

I don't remember now how many people were added to the faith as a result of that series. It must have been about half a dozen or so, but I experienced for the first time the joy of working with people and seeing them go down into the water with Jesus. Up to today, I still say that there is hardly any surpassing joy.

But I cannot fail to tell you of an absolute miracle that took place during the run-up to that series of meetings.

One Sunday afternoon, a group of us numbering about ten or twelve bundled into an old Datsun pickup truck and headed to the neighbouring village of Calibishie to give Bible studies and invite people to the meetings. Under normal circumstances we would not have driven that vehicle because it was simply not roadworthy: the body was literally falling apart due to advanced rusting and it had no functioning headlamps. But that was the only mode of transport available to us that day. So we agreed to take our chances—leave for Calibishie around 3:00 p.m., get through our visitation within a couple of hours, and head back home before nightfall.

Well, some members of the team simply did not know how to cut their visits short, so by the time we all returned to the rendezvous point, it was already dark! Yep; it was dark. I saw trouble coming. The prospect of driving that old Datsun home in the near-total darkness of our country roads was not an exciting one. But again, we had no choice. We simply had to go.

Just then, someone came up with a bright idea.

"Hey, here's a flashlight!"

Ha! A flashlight! A pretty bright idea, pardon the pun; won't you agree? But it was better than anything we had, which was... nothing. The suggestion was for someone to stand just behind the cab and shine the light while the driver would go as slowly as he could.

"What?"

"Yes. End of discussion. Let's go!"

"No; let's pray."

This time there was no discussion, only unanimous agreement. So we all prayed for God's protection, climbed into the Datsun, and started making our way slowly down the road.

We had just gone past the last village light when we spotted the headlights of a car coming toward us in the opposite direction. As it drew nearer, we were thrilled with the extra light it provided momentarily. But then it passed, and as it did, we expected to return to the semi-darkness of our little flashlight. But the opposite happened. The road ahead remained bathed in a bright mysterious light that seemed to come FROM our Datsun! It almost seemed as if the passing car had lent us some of its light. We were amazed beyond description. We were so ecstatic, so overjoyed that we could not stop chattering and laughing all the way home.

Actually, it was when we got home that the magnitude of this miracle really hit us, for as soon as the driver switched off the engine, the lights went dead. He tried several times to turn them back on but to no avail. That was it. In fact, after that amazing experience, the old Datsun remained parked away for good and was eventually sold by parts.

Phew!

Whenever I think about it, I'm simply left shaking my head. It's as if God had gone the distance to say to our group (and to me), "Hey, I love what you're doing and I am with you." He should have gotten my full attention then, but …Oh well! I guess I wasn't paying Him any.

A few years later, I was again asked to preach in an evangelistic series in Calibishie. I thought, "Hm! Why not?" I was getting hooked on to this preaching stuff, it seemed, and I was absolutely sure that the God who had blessed us earlier would grant at least the same measure of blessing for round two. So I said yes. Let's go!

But unlike my first home-based series, which was conducted in the spaciousness of our church building, we had no place large enough to accommodate the anticipated turnout, so we decided to pitch a tent. We found a piece of land almost in the middle of the village and just a few steps from the little rented house where we used to meet for worship, but given the size of our tent, that plot of land proved to be far too small. So we decided to ask the owners of the adjoining piece of land if we could extend our tent into their property. Initially, they were reluctant to have their land used for that purpose, since they were of another religious persuasion, but we prayed and God heard, and the hand of Omnipotence moved things in our favor. They gave us permission.

So we pitched our tent and for the next five weeks, five nights a week, we presented the truths of God's word. By then, I was a much more seasoned preacher. The sermons were still not of my own making, but I had lost my boyish voice, didn't need to stand on crates anymore, and had gotten the hang of ending properly—not with that infamous line. At the end of that series, we had many more baptisms, including several members of one family.

All praise and glory be to God!

But watch this: as an icing on the cake, the very plot of land on which the tent stood was put up for sale and, since we were already there, we got preferential consideration and were able to buy the land for the erection of a new church building. That building is still standing today. Hallelujah!

The Calibishie congregation was growing and needed nurturing, so the leaders at Bense church asked me to partner with the evangelism coordinator, Brother Francois (now deceased), in meeting this need. Almost every week for the next few years, I spent all day Saturday as well as two hours every Sunday and Wednesday evening with that little flock, preaching, teaching, training and nurturing them. Calibishie became my second home. As I trudged up and down the hills and along the bayside flat doing Bible studies and home visitations, I became quite a familiar face in the place. People knew me either because of what I was doing or because of who I looked like—my father. So I had more than one reason to walk circumspectly.

My activities caught the eye of several leaders of other Christian congregations in the community, and one day the pastor of the Baptist congregation personally approached me and suggested that I should go to study for the ministry. That was a pleasant surprise. Sure, we chatted about it for a few minutes, at the end of which I thanked him for his kind words and promised to give it some thought. But to be honest, I went away feeling, "Hey, that's not for me. I don't feel called to pastoral ministry. Besides, I'm quite happy doing what I'm doing."

That, my dear reader, would be the ready-made answer I gave to everyone who thereafter threw that suggestion at me over the next sixteen years. For me, suggestion minus conviction equalled only one thing: it wasn't from God. I'm not saying my interpretation was right; I'm only telling you what happened. Now, I know otherwise.

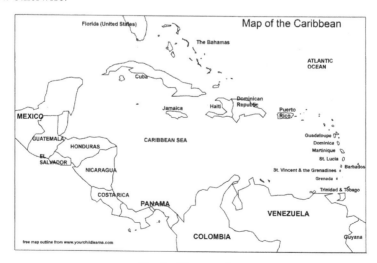

The Caribbean region

Life as I knew it took a short turn when from 1983 to 1984 I went to France on a scholarship to pursue a university diploma for foreign teachers of the French language. There, I lived in Vichy, a city located in the very centre of France, a city famous for its mineral waters and thermal baths as well as its historical significance: it served as the seat of French government during the Nazi occupation of World War II. In Vichy I found a small Adventist congregation and began worshiping with them. By the end of the second week they had unofficially appointed me to serve as their organist since there was nobody to accompany the singing at church services. The kind pastor gave me, still a total stranger, a key to the church building so that I could go there and practice whenever I wanted. He also invited me to preach once. That was pretty daunting, but I put on a brave face and accepted. Daring not to leave anything to chance and remembering my first day in the pulpit, I scripted every word of that sermon! Every word! And although I was pretty confident, I worked up a decent sweat that cold morning. But again, the saints were very sympathetic—as saints should be; they all said "Amen."

I returned to Dominica in mid-1984 and for the next 3 years I remained busy with my teaching job while serving in various positions of responsibility in Adventist youth work on my island. Undoubtedly, the greatest one was that of President of the Adventist Youth Council (AYC), an island-wide umbrella organization for youth ministry. I must have been just eighteen or nineteen when that mantle was first placed on my shoulders, and I eventually served for two terms.

Look! I really had no idea what those folks saw in me that caused them to select and elect me. I was just absolutely clueless. Why did I accept it? I guess it's because I was just being me: someone who had never learned to say "No" to church-related duties, someone who was taught to embrace every opportunity to use his talents for God's glory, and someone who always felt quite happy making people always feel quite happy. With societies, leadership teams, and events scattered all around the island, leading the AYC was tough; it involved much travelling around, many meetings and several major events, such as youth conventions and camps, each year; but I was blessed with a corps of very committed, efficient associates who made my work much easier.

## *Delivered from the Deep*

In the summer of 1985, while I was still AYC President, I lived through an experience which taught me to appreciate life and to cherish the opportunity God later gave me to hear and respond to His call. That year, the annual conference-wide youth camp was held on the neighbouring island of St. Lucia. Since youth camp was a major event, something every young person looked forward to attending, the AYC came up with a plan to help as many youth as possible to realize their dream: we would charter a boat, thereby significantly reducing the cost of getting to and from St. Lucia.

The plan worked! About sixty-four persons signed up for camp, of which fifty-four decided to take the boat trip. That was a huge success. For the first time,

Dominican campers were the largest nationality group at a camp held away from home. We literally flooded the camp!

Now, in today's age of budget airlines and factory discounts, many people have learned that to enjoy lower prices you have to put up with some degree of inconvenience. And that's exactly what happened to us. Because of the boat's schedule, we were forced to arrive in St. Lucia three days before camp and leave five days after, so we had our own little pre-camp camp and post-camp camp. That was the price for cheaper fares. Fortunately, the management of the Adventist Academy, where we camped, was gracious enough to let us stay the extra time without charges.

Camp came and went in the blink of an eye and before we knew it, the day arrived when we were to set sail from St. Lucia on our return to Dominica. Ours was a midnight departure, so nobody went to bed that evening. We arrived at the pier to find a crew of sailors who, though seasoned in their trade, were seriously concerned about the dire conditions they had just encountered but stressed that they couldn't wait until the sea calmed down since they had to head further north to the Virgin Islands the following day. I remember asking one,

"How's the sea?"

He answered, "Boy, I've seen rough seas, but this one is really bad. I have never seen anything like this before."

My heart sank like a rock dropped in the ocean. I felt like we were about to be taken on a death ride. Some fifty young people on my account! Oh Lord! And as if the harrowing prospect before us were not enough, one camper slipped and fell off the edge of the pier into the dark water below as she was trying to help load the luggage onto the boat. We pulled her out safely, but that felt pretty ominous, I must admit.

Well, after a fervent prayer to God for "travelling mercies" (pardon the cliché) we boarded the old retired trawler named *Miss Orva* and cast off on the stroke of midnight. No sooner had we rounded the headland than we found that the usually calm waters of the Caribbean Sea, which bathes the island's leeward coast, were exceedingly choppy. So choppy were they, in fact, that those who had taken up comfortable positions at the boat's stern were forced to flee for shelter nearer the front. Some campers decided that the best way to face our danger was to sing, so we began singing as courageously as we could. Needless to say, as the journey became more perilous, the songs died away; every one resorted to seeking their own place of refuge and awaiting the worst.

We soon passed the northernmost point of St. Lucia and headed out into the open channel which separates it from the French island of Martinique. That was when all hell seemed to have broken loose! No longer under the shelter of the mountains, we were exposed to the fury of the north-easterly winds and the never-ending succession of swells which they churned up. Peering into the near pitch-blackness of the early morning hours, we could barely discern the white foaming wave crests racing toward the boat, threatening to break over its side and wash us all overboard. They always seemed to be higher than the boat itself, so I routinely found myself wondering, "Oh Lord! Are we going to make it? Is the boat going to ride this one?" And each time, thank God, the boat climbed, albeit at a perilous angle, and dropped sharply down the other side of the wave, only to prepare for the next one, while the one we had just ridden quickly raced away into the dark distance. Sometimes they came, three, four or five in rapid succession. The angry wind kept howling over and around us. At one point, it was so strong that a tarpaulin which was sheltering us was ripped in two from the back all the way to the front, as if by some incredibly strong pair of superhuman hands. And all the while, what do you think was happening? You guessed right: folks were just emptying the contents of their stomachs wherever they could. What an absolute mess! What could we do in such circumstances but just literally hang in there, go with the flow, and hope for the best? What could we do but take our eyes off the storm, look to the One who was ultimately in control of the elements, and wait on Him even "more than those who watch for the morning?" (Psalm 130:6)

We enjoyed a brief respite as we sailed past Martinique, but by six o'clock, when night had given way to the grey skies of a stormy morning, we were well and truly back in the thick of things as we negotiated the equally dangerous passage across to Dominica. The only difference was that now we could see the open waters and, for a limited time, the outline of the two islands.

By the time we landed on Dominica, It had been ten dreadful hours at sea. At the port, anxious parents and family members rejoiced to see us. We were tired, hungry and nauseated; our half dried clothes reeked of diesel and vomit, our faces and arms were half white with salt from evaporated sea spray, but thank God, we had survived. We were alive!

In the midst of our harrowing journey, I couldn't help but remember the words of the psalmist:

Those who go down to the sea in ships,
> Who do business on great waters,

They see the works of the LORD,
> And His wonders in the deep.

For He commands and raises the stormy wind,
> Which lifts up the waves of the sea.

They mount up to the heavens,
> They go down again to the depths;
> Their soul melts because of trouble.

They reel to and fro, and stagger like a drunken man,
> And are at their wits' end.

Then they cry out to the LORD in their trouble,
> And He brings them out of their distresses.

He calms the storm,
> So that its waves are still.

Then they are glad because they are quiet;
> So He guides them to their desired haven.

Oh, that men would give thanks to the LORD for His goodness,
> And for His wonderful works to the children of men! Psalm 107:23-31.

Now, as I look back on this episode, I'm deeply grateful that God took me through a "death ride" and allowed me to live, and I'm absolutely sure that it's because He had a plan for my life. There was something that He wanted me to do, something that I had not yet accepted to do. He had been calling, but I had not yet answered; He had been knocking on my door, but I had not yet opened it.

## *Reining the Rain—Again!*

In 1986, I again saw the hand of God at work, controlling the elements for His purpose. That year, all the churches across Dominica came together for an eight-week series of evangelistic meetings which were conducted under a huge tent pitched on a playing field near the main hospital in Roseau. Before the meetings began, we were encouraged to pray that God would grant us good weather so that many people could attend. This we did: we prayed and fasted.

And guess what. For eight weeks…! For eight long weeks, not a single drop of rain fell (except for a light shower one Saturday night when there was no meeting). For eight weeks, we drove for about seventy minutes from my home village to the tent meetings, returning home at almost eleven every night, much to the relief of my parents.

It felt like a mini drought. The grass everywhere turned brown. The trees shed their leaves as if autumn had suddenly been added to the Caribbean's seasonal calendar. The streams started running low on water, like those in Elijah's days. By the end of the meetings, we had baptized some five hundred people, most of them being new converts to the faith. That was something unheard of in Dominica up to that point. What a blessing!

But hold on. We concluded the meetings on a Saturday afternoon and spent most of Sunday taking the tent down. That very Sunday night, all the fountains of heaven seemed to have opened up. The rain came down with an attitude. It rained and rained. It poured and poured. It thundered. It showered as though the skies wanted to make up for having withheld their blessings from the earth for so long. "What a God," I thought! And from that very day I began to believe that truly, nothing is impossible with God. But more than that, in the context of my story, it was another of those jaw-dropping manifestations from God, another of those extraordinary events through which He was trying to say something to me.

Tent meeting in progress, April 1986

## *Training in Trinidad*

In 1987, I left home to attend Caribbean Union College (then CUC, now University of the Southern Caribbean) in Trinidad. That was a major turning point in my life. It was a milestone, indeed. Leaving for CUC was tantamount to flying out of the safety of the nest, returning only to spend a few weeks of school holidays. That's was my coming-of-age move, my rite of passage, so to speak. I had to swim or sink in an environment which was well known to either make or break a youngster.

CUC was different—very different from the small, simple, homogeneous country church of my formative years. From the first day I went to church I realized that it was easy to be lost in this complex multinational crowd which represented the best of the very best of many churches all around the Caribbean and indeed further afield. I concluded that unless I took the initiative to become an active participant in the spiritual life of the campus, I could simply lose my flame and end up gathering dust in some obscure and impersonal corner called "Study, Study, Study!"

So as soon as I could, I became involved in various forms of ministry, especially in music. I had bought a trumpet from my brother a few years earlier; that secured me a permanent seat in the college band. And because my rudimentarily musical dad had taught me to sing bass from the ripe old age of seven (that...! is another story!), I also found a permanent seat in the college choir. By the time of my graduation, I was singing bass in four different choirs both on and off campus. I also played the organ for church services on alternate Sabbaths. You should have seen my rehearsal schedule! Crazy! But it's the sort of thing one does when he is still single. Besides, I enjoyed the experience, especially going on church tours with The Collegiates, my all-time favourite chorale, and providing music for large occasions such as Alumni Weekend and Graduation.

At CUC I also joined a very vibrant Sabbath School group which... you can almost guess it... appointed me to be its leader for a couple of years. We were not simply content to meet together for study on Sabbath mornings; we also stretched our wings by ministering to nearby congregations, one of which would later become my adopted home church for a couple of years.

But I didn't preach.

Nope, I didn't.

Among preachers? I was not a preacher.

The preachers were the Theology majors. They carried their majors the way they carried their Bibles: with an air, tucked almost under their armpits with their elbows sticking out. They strutted it. They honed their homiletic skills while scrubbing themselves in the showers for unduly long periods on Friday evenings, trying to imitate as closely as they could the grunts, shouts and intonations of famous Black American preachers from Martin Luther King Jr to Barry Black, while their friends shouted Amens from adjacent showers and toilet cubicles. Then in their fourth year, they put their best feet forward for the Students' Weeks of Prayer when finally, they got their turn to show the rest of the campus community what the churches out there were in for.

No, I was no preacher. I didn't even try to preach.

So I don't understand why, in spite of all of this, people on the campus still thought that I was a theology major. And they were actually surprised when I told them I wasn't.

Graduating from CUC, 1991

So it was 1991: the year America invaded Iraq under the code name Operation Desert Storm; the year the Soviet Union crumbled; the year after the year Nelson Mandela walked free, ending twenty-seven years in prison. It was 1991, my final undergraduate year at CUC. There I was, lying on my bunk bed early one spring morning, drowsy but wide awake. And the story which you now know—the story of the dean knocking on my door—unfolded.

Now, you be the judge. Tell me: Was that the call?

You're probably saying "Yes," and now that I've had years to think about it, I have concluded that you're absolutely right. That early morning knock was not simply the dean's knock; it must have come from heaven.

Frankly, I don't feel good about saying this because it means, after all, that for the umpteenth time I had missed a golden opportunity. But still, I thank God for His patience and for His grace because... I tell you, if I were in God's place, I would have given up on calling Erickson. I'm thankful that His persistence outlasted my deafness. I'm grateful that He kept calling and calling, offering me more and even more opportunities to recognize His voice.

In 1993, two years after my early morning call through the dean, God planted me in a small church a few minutes down the road from CUC and a literal stone's throw from my new home. By then, I had just married a gorgeous young woman whom I had met for the first time in 1988 but who, for most of my time on the campus, was just another face in the place. Things had changed radically when I graduated and found myself working as a young faculty member, side by side with Jacqueline "Jackie" Remy, who in those days served as Administrative Assistant in the Office of Admissions and Records. So, long story short, we got married in July 1993 and set up home next to that little church perched on the hillside—the College Spark Church, so named because it had been founded many years earlier by staff and students of CUC.

No sooner had I settled in than I was appointed to serve as Youth Leader. I also played the piano for all church services and started a small choir.

Ok. Fine! That was enough for me.

But there was more to come. The next year, 1994, I was appointed as an elder. By the end of that year, the head elder declared that he needed a break from his role and would therefore be unavailable for 1995. So guess who was asked to replace him.

Me!

*Moi!*

I who for many years had vowed never to sit on a church board, let alone chair one; I who believed that too many head elders exercised too much power over their congregations; I who am naturally more spontaneous and scatter-brained that meticulous and methodical; I found myself arguing with myself in the face of a request that threatened to pull the threads and unravel the warm, cosy blanket of my decades-old comfort zone. Should I say yes? Should I decline?

Now being the head elder of a congregation, in case you didn't know it, is like being an assistant to the pastor. In fact, the head elder is the resident pastor in many instances where pastors have large church districts.

I could have said no. I could have run from the call as I had so often done in the past. But something convinced me that this was the time to stand up and be counted, at least at that level. Something told me that no was not the answer that would please God.

So I said yes.

I wish I could impress you by saying that I prayed and fasted and prayed some more before saying yes, but I don't think I did. I debated with myself, most likely talked to my wife about it, and then decided I would give it a shot.

And there I was, the pastor's assistant, the man on the ground when the pastor was unavailable, which was often enough.

The pastor himself, a tall, bald ethnic Indian man with a highly resonating voice and a speaking style more suited to someone twenty years younger, realized that I had not yet been set aside for this ministry as the manner of the church is; thus he decided to ordain me.

Now things were really beginning to get serious. I was not just a leader; I was the ordained head elder! That felt as if a weight of some significant magnitude had been dropped onto my shoulders, but it proved to be "a shadow of things to come" (a phrase found in Colossians 2:16) sixteen years later.

I spent the next year obtaining vital experience in unofficial pastoral ministry. That included preaching, holding Bible studies, chairing committee meetings, and conducting special services like baby dedication and communion. However, much of my time and energy went into home visitation. The head deacon and I spent a few hours every Wednesday and Thursday afternoon knocking on doors, irrespective of the religious affiliation of those inside, building stronger ties between the little congregation and the community. I really enjoyed it. Believe me, I was truly blessed.

Outside College Spark Church, 1994

## *Educational Experiences*

By now, you might be expecting me to admit that finally, I had recognized my calling. No! I had not. Not yet. It would take another seven years, during which a number of things happened in my life.

First, my aspirations and plans for doing a Master's degree in Teaching English as a Second Language (TESL) or Teaching English to Speakers of Other Languages (TESOL) utterly failed. At that time, I thought it was just misfortune; now, I think God foiled them because He had other plans. I had my eyes focused on getting my degree from either Florida International University or University of Puerto Rico, Mayaguez Campus; then I would go to teach English in some distant country like Saudi Arabia or Korea where English was always in demand and where the money was good. Those were my selfish plans. No wonder God frustrated them.

Then I got another reason to stay grounded: my wife was expecting our first child. Our daughter Annique was born on Christmas Day of 1995, just a couple of months after I gave up trying to get into a TESOL program. Her arrival was a source of great joy to us both. The feeling of holding one's firstborn, looking into her eyes and coming to terms with the miracle that has just occurred, is something one experiences only once in an entire lifetime, right?

Just before Annique was born, the East Caribbean Conference, which oversaw the work of the Adventist Church on the islands of Dominica, St. Lucia, Barbados, and St. Vincent and the Grenadines, appointed me to serve as Principal of the Bense Adventist Primary School. I was called back to my roots—Bense Church, which is where the school was based—and I accepted. So much for my lofty TESOL plans!

Thus, in January 1996, I left Trinidad after eight rather busy years to return to Dominica. I left my wife and eleven-day-old daughter behind; they would join me three months later. I will never forget the feeling of taking off in the little inter-island commuter plane for the last time in a long time. Nor can I ever forget the feeling of walking into that primary school on the morning of January 8, 1996 and having all those eager little eyes watching me as their new principal and addressing me as "Sir" and "Mr. Fabien!"

I was back at my early training ground, that place where I heard the earliest knocks on my door, that place where I was taught to say Samuel's words as a memory verse in Sabbath School, "Speak, Lord, for thy servant heareth." I was back playing the piano, leading the choir which I started, preaching, directing the AY programs, and teaching the Sabbath School classes. I was back going to Calibishie, though not as often, since by then it was a full-fledged church. Life had gone around in a full circle; I had returned.

I spent the next five years at Bense. School administration was different but not difficult. I think I learned fast enough. The school was well supported by four other churches, its examination results were quite good, and the morale among parents and teachers was quite healthy, but the finances were challenging. So in 1998, the year our son Christopher was born, we agreed after some negotiation to merge with another Adventist School which was located about twenty minutes away and which had its own share of challenges; that way, we felt we could enjoy greater economies of scale. That worked out quite well in the end, but like the hymn says, "It took a miracle!"

The challenge was finding a piece of land for the new school. We needed a central location so that the constituents of one school would not suffer an obvious disadvantage and thus be discouraged from supporting the new institution. It so happened that the other school, named Mariley because it was operated by the churches of Marigot and Wesley, had approximately one acre of agricultural land that the government wanted to take over as part of their plans to build a larger airport in the area. So with some hesitation, the management of Mariley School basically said to the government, "If you want our land, we don't mind giving it up; just give us another piece of land in exchange." And the government agreed.

Fantastic, you're thinking; but the best part is yet to come. Instead of an acre-for-acre swap, the new school was gifted five acres of relatively flat arable land! Five acres for one! Talk about blessings! The only fault was that it was located much closer to the Mariley School than to Bense, which meant that the Bense students would have to travel over a much greater distance. But in the end we all embraced it as a generous gift from God.

When I walked onto that piece of land for the first time, I could not imagine that we were about to build a school there. All I saw was forest: thick, overgrown tropical bush, trees competing for space and sunlight... just bush. It made no sense to me. The place was isolated. There was no access road, no water mains or electricity lines nearby, nothing that said, "Hey, this is an ideal spot for a primary school." But the pastor and elders who accompanied me that day were looking through the eye of faith, and as we got near the spot earmarked for the building, we stood in a circle and prayed that God would bless that place for His glory! And bless He did!

Over the next few months, things happened in rapid succession. Two of our elders were members of Marantha Volunteers International, an American-based non-profit Adventist organization whose members travel to various countries building churches and schools on a voluntary basis. These elders secured Maranatha's commitment to erecting a school building and having it fully ready in time for the start of the 1999-2000 school year. They were prepared to come to Dominica in late January or early February of 1999, so we were left with just a few months to clear the dense forest, build an access road, and lay the foundation in order that Maranatha could simply put up the structure, as was their custom.

It was clearly a race against time. But the churches rallied together, and for several consecutive Sundays we bent our backs into what became known as Operation Bush Push! The men came out with their chainsaws, axes and machetes, buzzing, chopping, and slashing, while a crew of women brought along their pots, pans and provisions, cooking up a storm. And those who were neither choppers of wood nor cookers of food cleared whatever was chopped and ate whatever was cooked. Before we knew it, the jungle was gone!

Then came the challenge of building the road so that construction materials could be transported to the site for laying the foundation. But there was a major problem: we were still in the rainy season, and the almost incessant downpours made it too difficult and dangerous to operate a bulldozer on the slopes leading up to the property. All we could do was pray for favourable weather.

So we prayed and prayed, but alas, it kept raining and raining. It seemed like there would be no end to the showers. It seemed, too, that God was testing our faith to its very limit. Each anxious passing day meant that the foundation was being delayed. We just kept praying... and waiting... and...yes!

Just in the nick of time, just when it seemed we were going to miss the Maranatha deadline, just when we needed it most, the rains stopped. The sun came out in all its blazing glory. The bulldozer went to work. The road was built. Praise God! He came through on time. (God always comes through on time.)

Maranatha Volunteers arrived a few weeks later to find a completed foundation. With the same energy they had pumped into Operation Bush Push, the members turned out to work side by side with our overseas volunteers. Like in the days of Nehemiah, "we built the [school]... for the people had a mind to work" (Nehemiah 4:6). The new school, named Temple Seventh-day Adventist Primary School because of its location on Temple Estate, was finished and furnished, ready for the start of the 1999-2000 school year.

Temple School under construction

Speaking at the school's official opening, the country's Prime Minister stated that if anyone had told him a few months earlier that a new school would be opened on that spot on such and such a date, he would have thought it almost impossible. Calling it a miracle, he heaped generous praise on the church community for making it happen. That sounded good, but we all knew we couldn't take the credit. Without the wonder-working power of Almighty God, the script would not have read so beautifully. All praise and glory to Him!!

I served as Temple School's principal for its inaugural academic year and for the first term of its second year. During that term, the Education Department of the East Caribbean Conference called me to serve as Principal of our secondary school on the island of Bequia (pronounced beck-way), part of the St. Vincent and the Grenadines archipelago. At first I declined the invitation because my wife had just started working again after five years, and our daughter had just started her first term of school. But the call came a second time, and this time, after some consultation with God and Jackie, I decided to accept it. And so it was, that as dawn broke over the New Year 2001, we found ourselves once more starting a new life in a new role among new people.

Our move to Bequia proved to be a blessing of untold proportions. If I were to summarize its significance, I would say it literally changed the entire course of the rest of my life. For it was on that little gem of an island that I finally recognized and answered the call of God. "It was there, by faith, I received my sight"—a vision of what God had in store for me. It was there that a series of amazing events began to unfold before my eyes. In fact, if I had not gone to Bequia, I would in all probability not be sitting here writing this story.

Enough said.

We've just finished a long and eventful journey starting at Bense, my home village, winding through several other Dominican communities, pausing in France, then stopping over in Trinidad and Tobago for eight years before finally returning to Bense. Along the way we have witnessed several amazing miracles—trail markers dropped by an all-seeing and exceedingly patient God who was simply trying to say, "This is the way; walk in it" (Isaiah 30:21). And failing to hear the voice or discern the signs, I, like Samuel went back to sleep each time.

But hang on: we've only just begun. Where you've just been is nothing compared to where you're going. So come with me. I'm about to take you on a hair-raising adventure with God.

# III

# THE TURNING POINT

> *So Gideon said to God, "If You will save Israel by my hand as You have said—look, I shall put a fleece of wool on the threshing floor; if there is dew on the fleece only, and it is dry on all the ground, then I shall know that You will save Israel by my hand, as You have said." And it was so. When he rose early the next morning and squeezed the fleece together, he wrung the dew out of the fleece, a bowlful of water. Then Gideon said to God, "Do not be angry with me, but let me speak just once more: Let me test, I pray, just once more with the fleece; let it now be dry only on the fleece, but on all the ground let there be dew." And God did so that night. It was dry on the fleece only, but there was dew on all the ground. Judges 6:36-40*

*Prologue*

It's six fifty-nine on a glorious Sunday morning in May, 2003. I've just settled into a chair on the porch of my temporary home on the western slopes of a small tropical island. On a little table to my left is my breakfast: a bowl filled with a multicoloured mixture of raisin bran, corn flakes and granola, all soaked down with milk, and a few slices of whole wheat toast smeared evenly but lightly with peanut butter.

The sunshine is bright but the air is still cool. Various species of birds dart from tree to tree as if on cue, calling noisily as they chase each other. Amid their music I can hear waves gently lapping the shoreline down on the two beaches which are but a short walk in either direction from my front door.

Jackie and the children are up but not yet out. I've just decided to have an earlier-than-usual Sunday morning start. And for me, it always starts with a hearty breakfast.

No sooner do I start to munch on the first few spoons of my favourite cereal mix than I hear the familiar blaring of a ship's horn coming from the harbour far off to my right. And although I've watched this happen day after day for the last several weeks, I leave my breakfast chair and walk forward, leaning curiously over the railing to catch a better, less obstructed view.

Over in the harbour, probably less than a kilometre away, a few dinghies, two or three water taxis, and a bright yellow service craft bearing the words "Ice, Laundry, Water, Diesel," are scurrying around while dozens of yachts from all around the world sit idly in the morning's golden sun, their masts occasionally deviating from the vertical as miniature swells generated by those lesser boats reach them. Then out of the right-hand corner appears a much larger vessel, the source of the blaring that had distracted me from my breakfast. Its white-atop-red colours identify it as belonging to the Bequia Express fleet, owned and operated by one of the two ferry enterprises on the island.

I watch as it gathers speed, sailing gracefully toward the headland below the ruins of an ancient fort. Rounding the point, it disappears into the distance where the perennial placidity of the Caribbean Sea surrenders to the surges and swells of the Atlantic, leaving in its wake an ever-widening arrowhead of trails.

I return to my table. The corn flakes and raisin bran have lost their crispiness, but I don't mind; I've enjoyed watching the ferry leave. If I were overlooking an airport, I would just as readily have sacrificed a few minutes to watch an Airbus A330 or Boeing 777 land or takeoff.

I finish my breakfast and head inside. It's Sunday morning but there's work to be done in preparation for school tomorrow.

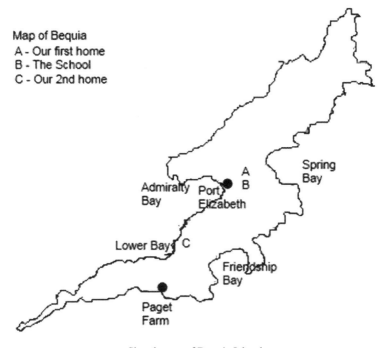

Sketch map of Bequia Island

Bequia Seventh-day Adventist Secondary School

## *Bequia Biddings*

Welcome to Bequia. By small island standards, this is the definition of a small island. It's only 7 square miles or 18 square kilometres big and is home to just about 4,300 people. If you are ever tempted to think that small is not beautiful, all you need to do is hop on a ferry or yacht and sail into Bequia's main harbour, Port Elizabeth; that's how most people get there anyway. The stunning view of green hills rising out of the deep blue, placid Caribbean Sea and outlining themselves against the idyllic mix of cotton-candy clouds and azure skies is enough to convert you. You will soon realize that if you ever needed to escape from the hustle and bustle of city life, this would have to be your sanctuary.

However, my family and I didn't go to Bequia on vacation. As I indicated earlier, I was asked to serve as Principal of the Bequia Seventh-day Adventist Secondary School. On the surface, it was nothing more and nothing else, but in retrospect, I'd say it was an intentional move on God's part. It was but one more stroke of the pen in His grand design.

On Bequia, I did that which I had always known myself to do: I immediately became involved in the ministries of the Port Elizabeth congregation, including music and worship (I started a choir—again!), preaching, Sabbath School, Men's Fellowship, and the Adventist Youth Society. My wife also threw her energy into the children's Sabbath School and the Women's Ministry. The believers there welcomed us very warmly and were quite happy with our participation.

I recall with joy the hours spent in door-to-door visitation, inviting people to attend an evangelistic program or to donate to the annual fundraising drive traditionally known as Ingathering. I recall the many evenings spent under the canvass tent on the island's southern side, playing the "singing evangelist's" role and loudly affirming the preacher as he delivered the word with power. I remember teaming up with a trio called D-Ziah and playing keyboards for a band named "Vision." I remember, too, trekking up and down the hills to visit parishioners in the convenience of their homes. I was busy with my administrative responsibilities at the school but I was equally taken up with ministry tasks at the church. And I loved it. And I'll always think back with fond memories of those two and a half years.

But the pivotal point, the moment that changed everything, came during a chat Jackie and I had one evening in February of 2002. We just lay there one night "pillow-talking" like we often do at the end of the day before sleep overwhelms us, and she was sensing the tone of frustration in my voice over some issue at school, something which I no longer remember. But comparing my remarks with some I had made on another recent occasion, she asked me a searching question:

"Erickson, is that what you really want to do for the rest of your life?" While I searched for the right words to respond, she shot another pointed question: "What do you really love doing?" Then another: "What gives you a feeling of fulfilment every time you do it?" Then a fourth: "What do you feel you are really good at and you don't mind doing for the rest of your life."

I finally had a chance to respond. "You know! I love teaching, preaching, singing, encouraging, ministering..., stuff like that! I am in Administration, but I don't think it's my strong point."

"So why don't you consider the Ministry?"

Phew! What was that? I had heard it from many different people umpteen times and in as many places, but now it had come from the pillow right next to me!

She continued, "You teach well, you preach well, you reach people well, you have a way with the brethren, you sing very well...you know; you could probably combine all of those into a very successful ministry."

"Yeah... I've thought of that; but you know, I have always said that one should feel called to the Ministry, and I have never felt called."

There it was! I had excused myself again! To that, she might have said something like "Well, "Babes" (her favourite way of calling me), "think about it and ask God to show you;" and I must have promised to do so.

For the next few months, the idea went no further than an idea... except for one thing. I had practically gained entry into the Master of Arts (M.A.) program in Educational Administration at Antillean Adventist University in Puerto Rico and was really excited about commencing my studies that summer. In fact, my conference had already approved some measure of financial assistance for me toward that purpose. But since time was of the essence, I took the bold step of cancelling those arrangements. I then wrote to the director of the M.A. program and told her I had decided to pursue other career interests and would therefore no longer be coming. I also thankfully informed my conference leadership that I would no longer need its assistance. This was truly a turning point in favour of the eventual decision. There would be no turning back.

The 2001-2002 school year ended and we spent the entire summer vacation on Bequia, going to the school almost every day where my wife tried to improve the organization of the library as I sought to tie up ends and prepare for the next year. The weeks sped by and before we knew it September had dawned. I remember thinking in June about the reality that if I had not cancelled my plan, I would have been in Puerto Rico. But I did not regret my decision. I just felt that God would show me the other path that He had mapped out for me. And He did.

Just a few weeks into the new term, my former college president, Dr. Vernon E. Andrews, invited me to join him in Kingstown (capital of St. Vincent and the Grenadines) one Sabbath morning where he was scheduled to do several presentations on Music as part of a "School of Evangelism" conducted by the Caribbean Union Conference's Personal Ministries Department. I went, enjoyed a good morning of activities and had the pleasure of dining with the other presenters at a hotel on the south coast not far from Kingstown.

Sitting at the table right next to me was Pastor Caius Alfred of St. Lucia, then serving in St. Vincent, someone whom I had first met at CUC where we worked together in the food services department. I shared my Bequia experiences with Pastor Alfred, who showed great interest, especially in my recent activities and interactions with the people of that island. At one point he made the statement that I had heard in so many different ways in the past: "I think you would do well as a pastor."

You're probably shaking your head, exclaiming, "What? Again?"

Yes; again—like a repeated phrase from an old scratched vinyl record! *Déjà vu!* More like *déjà entendu* (heard before)!

I propped my left elbow on the table top and cradled my forehead in my left palm, dropping my head until my beard touched my tie and my fingers were able to clutch the back of my head—my classic nervous reaction. Then I quickly raised my head, looked back at him, and just let it out: I told him as much as I could remember of my fifteen-plus-year history of hearing similar remarks.

His next few words came straight as an arrow: "Brother, maybe God is calling you into the Ministry. Maybe He has been calling you for a long time and you have not recognized it. I think you should go home and pray about it, asking God to show you clearly if that is really the way He wants you to go. Ask for a sign."

Then Pastor Alfred proceeded to relate his own experience: he too had been a teacher and principal for several years but had heard the Lord's call and felt the Spirit's moving, urging him to go into the Ministry. He had prayed for a sign and the Lord had answered clearly and directly; consequently, he had left all and gone to CUC, where I first met him. He further related how God had helped him bring his family to Trinidad and take care of them there, to the point where his wife was able to pursue her own studies.

That Saturday evening I went home thinking about the conversation which had obviously been the highlight of my day. I decided there and then that I was going to follow my friend's advice and pray about it. At bedtime, during our usual pillow talk, I shared with my wife the day's events, especially my discussion with Pastor Alfred. She was quite pleased with my enthusiasm and we agreed there and then to pray together. We recognized that a move in the direction of the Ministry would be a life-changing one for the whole family, something which deserved nothing less than prayerful and careful consideration.

Sunday passed quickly and uneventfully, and soon it was Monday at three in the morning—the time when I usually got up for personal meditation and prayer. That morning I decided it was time to ask for a sign. Yep! I said, "Lord, you know I'm trying to make up my mind about what transpired on Saturday. You know I want to make the right decision. You know how I feel about being a pastor and you know that I have NEVER ever felt called in that direction. So Lord, if you really want me in pastoral ministry, you're gonna have to give me a clear sign. Have someone incorrectly call me 'Pastor' before this day is through."

That was it. I threw it at Him. The ball was in God's court.

Well, what do you know? The day passed normally and uneventfully, except for one thing: I got locked out of my office that afternoon. Thinking I had gone out with my bunch of keys, Mrs. Psyche Ollivierre, the secretary, locked the office and left for home around four as usual. When I returned to the school I found myself in a pretty awkward situation. I stood out there for a few minutes trying to decide what to do and feeling…well…disgusted with myself. Then I left for home; after all, what else could I do? But when I got home, I realized that indeed I had a task to complete at the office—something that really could not wait until the next day. For reasons I can no longer recall, it was impossible to reach the secretary by telephone, so I decided to go to her Mount Pleasant home by any available means.

I had almost reached the Bequia Community High School, just a short walk from my home, when I heard a call of "Pastor! Pastor!" Turning in the direction of the voice, I saw a young man from the area, someone who saw me every morning and evening going to and from work, and who therefore knew that I was no other than Principal of the Adventist Secondary School. He wanted me to tell his friend Lowell, who was at the far end of the playing field watching an ongoing football (soccer) match, to come across to meet him. I smiled, agreed, walked to where Lowell was, relayed the message, and continued on my way. Unfortunately, I ended up walking all the way to Mount Pleasant where I explained my plight to Psyche; she graciously lent me her keys and I returned to the school, finished my task and headed home.

That night, as I knelt in prayer beside my bed, something hit me like a bolt! My morning prayer!

God had answered! And He had answered just the way I had asked—that someone would call me "Pastor" before the end of the day!

Excitedly, I told Jackie the whole story. We both agreed this was nothing short of divine intervention and immediately sent up a prayer of thanks to heaven. That Monday night proved to be D-Night--the night which actually changed the course of our lives and set us out on a remarkable journey of faith.

Sometimes when you ask for one, God gives you two, as if to make a point. And that's what He did, loudly and clearly.

A few days later, I was standing across the street from Greaves Supermarket in Kingstown, waiting for someone who was making a purchase there before catching the ferry home. Earlier that day, I had attended a meeting of secondary school principals and officials from the Ministry of Education, so I was reasonably well dressed. Along the street toward me shuffled an old, seriously bent-over, elderly woman whom I had never seen before. She appeared as if from nowhere, tapping her walking stick against the pavement, dragging a pair of worn-out sandals, seemingly muttering something to herself. When she reached where I was standing she paused, lifted her bent frame as much as she could, looked toward me and called,

"Pastor!"

(I'm almost certain of it: you're shaking your head in disbelief as you're reading this.)

Imagine my shock!

"Who? Me?" I questioned, even if I knew there was no one else standing there with me.

"Aren't you Pastor Pope?" she inquired.

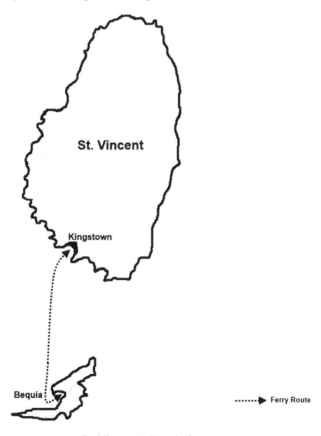

St. Vincent to Bequia ferry route

"Me? No ma'am," I answered, half bemused that this strange woman would come from God knows where... with, of all the possible questions in the world, this one!!!

"Are you a pastor?" she probed further.

"No ma'am; I'm not a pastor," I explained.

"Then maybe you should be one," she answered

(You're still shaking your head, reader.)

"You look like one," she concluded, resuming her toilsome journey, totally oblivious to what she had just done—or rather, what the Holy Spirit had just accomplished through her.

By now you're probably saying, like many others have said, "God truly moves in mysterious ways!" And yes; you're absolutely right. His ways are not only mysterious; they're also numberless.

## *Charting the Course*

Once we had concluded that this was what the Lord wanted me to do, Jackie and I immediately started discussing where we would go and how we would get there. In terms of where, the most obvious choice was CUC, our alma mater; the "how" was another matter (no pun intended).

CUC was a good choice for several reasons. First, it was home: Jackie is a Trinidadian and so is Annique. I had spent eight years of my young adult life there, studying, forming many precious friendships, and finally, getting married there. We would certainly have the support of family members; indeed, we would be quite at home. Second, we were still relatively well-known on the campus. Many of our formers colleagues in the various departments where we used to work were still around and had on numerous occasions asked us when we planned to return. This meant, thirdly, that supporting a family and studying would be feasible since we could very likely secure a job on or off campus. CUC was the comfort zone; CUC seemed to be the place.

Except for two things: One; we agreed that this move should not be a selfish one, catering for the husband while the wife just "tagged along". We analysed what we had seen in the lives of several pastoral couples and concluded that our move should be the kind that strengthened our marriage instead of weakening it. As I would grow, so should my wife. But as we looked, we could not find a program she could pursue based on her interests. And Two; going back to CUC meant I would have to complete another bachelor's degree. That's the best my alma mater had to offer by way of basic preparation for the Ministry. Frankly, approaching my fortieth birthday, I was not excited at the thought of completing another BA; I felt I should be moving upward in my educational pursuits, even if it were not simply for the sake of pursuing higher education.

So we began to look elsewhere. There was Northern Caribbean University, formerly West Indies College, in Jamaica, but on visiting its website I did not see what I wanted. I visited other sites, including Montemorelos University in Mexico and the ever-popular Andrews University in Michigan, but I could not decide in favor of these. I must have spent several hours surfing the internet, just looking at my options.

It was then that Jackie recalled the separate conversations we had had with Dr. Kenneth Mulzac in March of that year. Dr Mulzac, now deceased, had been visiting his island home of Bequia for several days. One afternoon he had stopped by the SDA Secondary School and had chatted separately with Jackie and me, telling us about this institution in the Philippines where he worked—some school with a very long name... Adventist International Institute of Advanced Studies (AIIAS), which he described as "the best kept secret in Adventist education." He had visited our home later that same day and spoken further with Jackie about the prospects of going there, leaving us a very enticing invitation: if we could come with at least our first semester's fees, he could guarantee that we would make it.

So that night I went online and visited AIIAS. It looked good. The photos were just so lovely, the course offerings were quite interesting, and the cost was so very affordable! As far as I could see, He was right.

Honestly, we appreciated the warmth and kindness of Dr. Mulzac. He was obviously a very nice person and AIIAS sounded like a great place; but the thought of going so far to study was just...well...so literally farfetched! The Philippines! For us, that's on the other side of the world, twelve time zones away! It would cost "an arm and a leg" to go there, and we could not even spare half an arm! So we had shelved the idea all these months.

But now, it was November. Having ruled out CUC, and knowing that education in the USA is quite costly, we were suddenly faced with the reality that AIIAS was our best option to date. Not that we had checked out all possible options; it's just that AIIAS looked really good!

But remember, we didn't have the money.

That's an understatement, really. I was due to travel to Dominica in December with my son Christopher to attend a cousin's wedding. At the same time, Jackie and Annique were due to fly to Trinidad for the Christmas holidays, and those two trips were going to cost us a tidy sum. In that context, and against the background of limited savings, going to the Philippines sounded downright crazy. Absolutely wild!

So I decided to pray. I did not tell Jackie; I wanted to do this myself. I just got up one morning and asked the Lord for a sign indicating whether He wanted us to go to the Philippines. And I got two!

Yes, God gives double blessings!

That month, we were in the midst of an evangelistic series being held under a large tent erected on the grounds at the southern end of the secondary school. Pastor Samuel Telemaque of the Caribbean Union Conference had announced there would be special guests that night, including Dr. Roy Adams, then Associate Editor of the Adventist Review, a native of neighbouring Grenada and an alumnus of CUC. I prayed in my very simple way, "Lord, if you think I should go to the Philippines, let that man say something, just anything, about being in the Philippines when he speaks tonight."

And the Lord heard.

Would you believe it? Before Dr. Adams got halfway into his speech, he related an experience he had had while visiting the Philippines. As the words escaped his lips, I found myself in my own little world, lost in wonder that God would actually answer my simplistic-sounding prayer.

I told Jackie about it but to be honest she was a bit sceptical. Initially, I was dead sure of what had happened but then her reaction left me feeling a bit shaky, and since I wanted to be "dead sure," I decided, like Gideon of old that a wet fleece wasn't quite enough. I needed something more: a dry fleece; another sign. So I asked, and here's what happened.

A few days thereafter I was supposed to attend a meeting in Kingstown. That morning as I prepared to leave home, I said, "Lord, if you really want me to go to the Philippines, just let me see the word 'Philippines' written somewhere during the course of the day." Again, that might sound rather silly to you, dear reader, but that's exactly what I prayed. I was dealing with a massive, life-changing issue and I really needed strong irrefutable evidence and clear guidance from God. So that was my prayer.

And the Lord heard.

As I was sailing northward on the Bequia Express ferry, I was positioned where I could see a small television screen on which the CNN morning news was being shown. I was not monitoring the screen at all; I was more interested in looking at the waves and just being alone with my thoughts. But at one point I suddenly raised my head in the direction of that little TV screen and there, on the red scrolling ticker bar at the bottom of the screen, I saw three words disappearing to the left. Just three words: "...in the Philippines!"

That was it. The next news headline followed quickly so I decided to wait a few minutes until that story about the Philippines would loop around, but it never came back. I got off the ferry, went to my meeting and returned home, still absolutely clueless regarding that mysterious news story. Twelve years later, I'm still clueless.

But that was all I needed. I had actually gotten another clue—a sign from above. God had confirmed it: we were going to the Philippines!

As soon as I got home I shared with my wife once more the good news of what God had done, and this time she was convinced. Her response was swift: she immediately went online, found the AIIAS website, downloaded the application package, printed the forms and together we went to work on them immediately. I was truly excited. I began reading up on the Philippines to see what I could learn. Interestingly, what stood out in my mind from this research were the jeepneys (modified jeeps used as a common mode of transport) and the Chocolate Hills, a geological formation in Bohol Province.

Yes, indeed; I was excited! We were all excited! But how would others deal with our departure? Where would we get the money, the "arm and leg" we needed for tickets, tuition and living expenses? We had quite a few hurdles to cross, but we were determined. We were going!

True to our plan, the family split for two weeks that December, the girls heading to Trinidad and the guys going to Dominica. While there, I told my parents about our decision. They were quite pleased to hear that I had made up my mind for the Ministry, but my mother's question was "Why so far?" I explained, and I think she understood, but it was clear to me that she wished we were thinking of somewhere closer. I also shared my decision with members of my home church and their response truly encouraged me. I will always remember Brother Jude Joseph, the first elder, approaching me at the piano shortly after the Adventist Youth service that second Sabbath afternoon and telling me he had always felt this is what I should be doing and he wondered why it had taken me so long.

The voice of the people, they say, is the voice of God!

On December 31, 2002, I left my parents and my home village knowing full well that this would be the last time in many years that I would be there. There was no doubt we were going, but by all indications it would be a journey of faith, not of sight.

# IV

# Forward In Faith

> *And Moses said to the people, "Do not be afraid. Stand still, and see the salvation of the Lord, which He will accomplish for you today. For the Egyptians whom you see today, you shall see again no more forever. The Lord will fight for you, and you shall hold your peace." And the Lord said to Moses, "Why do you cry to Me? Tell the children of Israel to go forward. But lift up your rod, and stretch out your hand over the sea and divide it. And the children of Israel shall go on dry ground through the midst of the sea. Exodus 14:13-16*

## Covering the Cost

We returned to Bequia on Old Year's night 2002 and very early in January we requested a bulletin from AIIAS because we felt we needed some more details. Meanwhile, we filled the forms, took photos, and sent the recommendation sheets to the referees we had chosen. The information downloaded from AIIAS's website had given us the impression that it was okay to apply in April for an October start, so there was really no need to rush things. However, when the bulletin arrived, we saw that our application ought to be received by the end of January!

When Jackie read the information to me, I panicked. I literally got an instant headache. My nerves got the better of me and I started pacing the floor. For the first time, I saw a huge obstacle in the way. Where would we find the almost four thousand United States dollars we needed for the application fee, international student deposit, and deposits for every additional family member?

I was seriously shaken but Jackie kept thinking, and then she said, "Well, let's pray." And pray we did. We dropped to our knees beside the bed that very moment and put the matter to God, each of us praying in turn.

When we got up, Jackie suggested that I work out a business plan with my father. The idea was that he could immediately help us make up the difference between what we had in hand and what we needed to send; then, over the next few months, from February to June, we would pay him back—interest free, of course.

Now I know my father, and I knew he would be willing to do that sort of thing for me. (You've got to know your father, folks.) So, just a few minutes after talking to my Heavenly Father, I got on the phone to my earthly father and put the matter to him.

Daddy was breathing heavily on the other end of the line, which told me it had finally dawned on him that I was serious about going to the distant Philippines; however, the man that I knew came to our rescue. Yes, he would send the money. He would go to the bank the very next morning and complete the transaction. Just like that! And so it was that in about a week or two, we were able to send our application and deposits on to AIIAS.

Now this business plan was not perfect. There was, in fact, a gaping hole right in the middle. You see, we had calculated that we would finish repaying my dad by the end of June and use whatever we earned in July to purchase our tickets to New York. It could work, but New York was NOT where we were heading; we were on our way to the Philippines, which was half a world further away. But we just felt somehow that all we needed to do was take the first step by getting to New York, and from there, God would open the way for us to complete the journey. That was the plan, the bold, daring, maybe-even-crazy plan.

Admittedly, I hate business risks and under normal circumstances I would never attempt something of that nature, but we were both absolutely sure that since God was with us, our plan would not fail. We knew it. We believed it. We were going forward by faith. From that point, Jackie started referring to the journey as "Our Red Sea Experience," but for me, it was like Abraham leaving his home for an unknown destination.

Recognizing that we should be constantly seeking God's face, we got down to praying as never before. One Friday we decided to have an extended evening worship session, devoting the extra time to study and prayer. Sundown worship was followed by the traditional Friday evening candlelight dinner; then we got the children ready for bed. For the next four hours or so thereafter, we spent time contemplating passages of scripture, singing a few hymns, and praying. We also found a lot of encouragement from Dr. Mulzac's book, "Praying With Power, Moving Mountains." The experiences he related therein really inspired us; after all, those things had happened in the life of someone we knew personally, and we concluded that if God did those for him, He could also do similar things for us.

Well, the first month, being February, passed very quickly and we had to make our first repayment to Daddy. When that was done and the bills had been paid, the harsh reality hit us smack in the face: we were going to have to live on a very tight budget for the next several months. That prospect looked extremely daunting. But right at the moment, Jackie came up with a second business plan: we would try to find another house or apartment where the rent was lower, thereby saving ourselves a couple hundreds of dollars each month. We would also cut off our telephone and internet service, which at the time cost enough to make a significant difference.

But where would we realistically find cheaper housing on Bequia? Hardly anywhere, for rent on Bequia was generally higher compared to the rest of St. Vincent and the Grenadines. Besides, we had already gotten a good deal on our current rented house. Still, we decided to ask around with sufficient secrecy so as not to cause a stir, so we checked about three people from our church who had space for rent. The list was quickly narrowed down to one, a brother with a vacant downstairs apartment about the same walking distance from the school as our present home, but in another direction. It was much cheaper, and it appeared the most likely resort except for a persistent water problem, especially in the dry season. We were almost at the point of taking it, but somehow we decided to wait one more week. I wanted something more from God, and I told my wife quite frankly that I was asking Him for the maximum, that is, zero dollars rent for the next four to five months!

Again, I know what you're thinking, but that was what my faith told me. I was totally confident that we could ask God for something really big instead of limiting Him to a couple hundreds. Jackie's reaction went something like this: "Well, brother, if that is your faith, go ahead. I guess God will have to go on your faith, because mine is not strong." Still, we agreed to pray about my request, holding on to the Bible promise that if any two persons agreed to pray together on any matter, God would grant the petition (Matthew 18:19).

I'm happy to testify that God kept His word, as He always does. All praise be to Him!

## *Fabulous Financial Favours*

As I indicated earlier, we had only one more week to make a decision, but that very Thursday afternoon something amazing happened. Jackie had to attend her weekly Women's Ministries meeting at the church, so I remained working at my desk expecting her to pass by when she was through. But a short while later, there she was, knocking on my office door and calling out to me. I opened the door, she stepped in, and as she began recounting what had happened at the church, her face lit up. Here's why.

Most of the group members had failed to turn up for the meeting, and that left her with only one other member, Sister Carmette Gooding, but they decided to have a prayer session anyway. They shared prayer requests and prayed, but after the prayer they began discussing Jackie's prayer request in some more detail.

All of a sudden, to Jackie's great surprise, Sister Gooding exclaimed, "But wait! You can stay at my place. It's not booked for the next four months, so you can stay there. Let me talk to my husband about it, and I'll let you know." Sure enough, she discussed the matter with her husband Frank, who agreed. We could stay at her guest apartment for the next four months; all we had to pay were the electricity and telephone bills, the use of which we could control.

It was almost incredible! I could not contain my joy. All I could keep saying was "God is good! God is good!"

**THROUGH MIRACLES TO MINISTRY**

I quickly informed our landlord, explaining to him in some detail why we were suddenly planning to leave the house. I felt God at work as the man stood there listening to me, for no sooner had I explained to him than he began telling me how he felt I was making the right decision. He was not an Adventist, he said, but he believed very strongly in all that Adventists stood for, having been a product and strong supporter of the very SDA Secondary School of which I was Principal. He further expressed his satisfaction with the way we had done business and how our family had related to him over the months. Then he made me an unforgettable promise: "Be sure to pass and visit me before you leave Bequia because there is something that I want to put in your hand. It may not be very big, but I believe it will help you." So whereas I had gone to him with some apprehension over what his response to our sudden decision could be, I left with his endorsement and a promise of some financial support, at least at the start. What more could I ask for?

On the night of Saturday March 29, 2003, we said goodbye to the house in Union Vale that had become home for the past two years and three months. Brother Frank Gooding came over with his pickup truck and helped us transfer our belongings to our new abode. I remember the curious gazes as we passed through the streets two or three times with the suitcases and other household effects piled high, while I sat at the back, holding on to whatever little space was left and making sure that nothing fell off unnoticed. It was quite an adventure.

We slept very briefly that night, having gone to bed pretty late. I recall waking up during the night and hearing the sound of waves gently breaking on the nearby beaches and thinking of how wonderful it would be to enjoy that sound every night for the next few months. The next morning we trekked along the beaches, hillsides, and streets, back to our former home to make one final cleaning so that it would be left absolutely bright and clean.

Our new temporary home was truly beautiful. Ideally situated a few steps away from the island's two most popular beaches, Lower Bay and Princess Margaret, it offered golden sunsets and a splendid panoramic view of the main harbor, Admiralty Bay. The ambience was quite relaxing, which was not surprising, seeing that it was an accommodation for foreign guests.

Whereas in the past we simply walked down the road for about 10 minutes to get to school, we now had to walk uphill to the north-south main road and catch a van going to "The Harbour", but we adjusted pretty quickly. Some mornings, as it was still cool, we simply made the twenty-five-minute trek along the seafront to school. The children were happy, even though they missed their Union Vale home with its plum and sugar apple trees.

It was around this time that we began explaining to Annique and Christopher what was really going on. Their reactions were mixed: they liked the idea of going to a new country far away and of seeing their cousins in New York in the process, but at the same time they did not like the fact that they would be parting ways with their friends on Bequia.

A couple of interesting things happened during those last four months. The first was that the SARS epidemic was raging in certain parts of Asia and in Toronto, Canada. Traveling to Asia was definitely risky business. In fact, a friend from the main island of St. Vincent who had left to study in Kuala Lumpur, Malaysia, was recalled because of the SARS threat. The death toll was mounting and I was concerned.

So one night I prayed, half asleep, half awake: "Lord, you have shown us that you want us to go to the Philippines, but what about SARS?" Almost before I could finish the question, a Bible verse rang in my ears: "You will not fear the terror of night, nor the arrow that flies by day, nor the pestilence that stalks in the darkness, nor the plague that destroys at midday" (Psalm 91:5 & 6, NIV). It was a straight case of "Don't worry; I am in control." Sure enough, by the time we were ready to leave Bequia, SARS was no longer a threat.

The second was that the Goodings had offered us their downstairs apartment but they had earlier planned to make some improvements to that section of the facility; so when they were ready they asked us kindly to move upstairs during the period of work. You might think this was an inconvenience but in actual fact, it was a blessing. By the time the work was through, we had just a few weeks left, so they allowed us to spend the remaining time in the much-more-spacious upstairs villa since that section was not booked until a couple of days after our scheduled date of departure. So really, their hospitality was way beyond what we had anticipated or even dared to imagine, and for that we will remain eternally grateful. I still do not know how to thank Brother and Sister Gooding but I know their reward will be great.

There is much more to say, for God gives in abundant measure. Spending those four rent-free months at that location truly allowed our business plan to work just fine. We were now able to make much larger monthly repayments to my father because of the savings we were realizing. And just when we had sent the second-to-last payment ... (sit tight!)...my father sent us a very welcome message: "It's ok. Don't send anymore."

I could hardly believe it! You see, my second eldest sister had earlier promised us a financial gift and at that point she declared that she was ready; in addition, my mother had decided to chip in with a gift too. The total of those two gifts was exactly the amount we needed to make the last repayment! So they paid Daddy and we kept our money. Unbelievable! Well, almost!

As if that were not enough, I received a call one day from the Executive Secretary of the East Caribbean Conference at its headquarters in Barbados. He was quite used to calling me, so I thought it was business as usual. But he went on to ask whether I was still planning to pursue my studies in the Philippines, because someone had told him I was no longer going. Of course, I was quick to correct that bit of misinformation. He then asked what had become of my request for financial assistance, to which I responded that it had not been approved. His next question was, "Are you still interested?" Of course, I was! So he instructed me to send the application in by such-and-such a date and address it to such-and-such a person, who incidentally was my immediate superior and who also chaired the committee which considers applications for educational assistance.

Now, I don't know what you would make of that conversation but it told me, "Erickson, you are definitely going to get financial assistance." So I quickly typed a letter and faxed it to the office in Barbados. A day or two later, I received via email a copy of the official form used for such applications and again, I filled it in and rushed it off.

Several weeks later, I called my immediate superior at headquarters and gently asked what the outcome was. Her response went something like this: "That was a foregone thing. I thought you knew." A big YES, in other words! There was one limitation, however: the assistance would cover only my tuition. It was less than I had hoped for but it was pretty good.

I pumped my fist in the air with another exuberant "Yes! God is good!" I would no longer have to worry about my tuition costs. I quickly found Jackie and shared the delightful news with her. That night, we had something really big to thank God for. Once more, He had shown us that He was right before us on this journey of faith, working things out for our good.

The 2002-2003 school year came to an end as quickly as it had arrived. I had to make several farewell speeches, including one at the annual graduation and awards ceremony and another at a staff farewell dinner held at a local pizza restaurant. We were soon on vacation and counting down the weeks, still going to the school most days to take care of our responsibilities. We wanted to make sure that everything would be left in order.

Meanwhile, I flew to Barbados to secure United States (US) visas for the children and myself only, since Jackie already had a valid one. (You might be wondering why we needed American visas since we were going to the Philippines. Well, it's simply because there are no direct flights between the Caribbean and the Philippines. Going through the US is the best option, and New York was a convenient transit point because we had close relatives and friends living there.)

Now obtaining an American visa in the Caribbean can be a very stressful thing. It's a hit-and-miss situation. You never really know if you will be successful and when you do succeed, it's like you've hit a lottery jackpot. I had applied for a US visa once before and was denied; this time, however, I was absolutely confident that we would all be successful. On the application form I was unable to correctly insert the address of the person with whom I would be staying in the US, but that did not bother me. I felt my case was sufficiently valid. I was on my way to the Philippines to study, as evidenced by my acceptance letter, my invitation letter, and a couple of other documents.

As I stood in line and later sat in the waiting area, I just kept thanking God for my success. I could see the disappointment on the faces of some who had just been interviewed and I couldn't help thinking, "If only they had things worked out the way I did!" Sure enough, I got the required visas although they were valid only for three months. My wife was a little disappointed at first, but then, thinking it over, we just had to thank God we got them after all. He had answered our specific request and He would take care of the rest.

On my visit to Barbados, I requested of the Conference treasurer that my July salary be sent early so we could tie up business ends and pay for our tickets to New York. We had applied for study leave effective July 31, 2003, which meant that we were not due August's salary. But imagine our surprise and delight when the envelopes came a few weeks later, containing the salaries not just for July but also for August. To make sure it was not an error, I called the office and got to speak with the Executive Secretary. He understood my concern but assured me that it was no error; rather, our employers had seen it fit to extend the courtesy by adding August's salary as well. Isn't God good?

But wait till you see what happened next. Based on what we had read in the AIIAS bulletin about getting visas for the Philippines, we had consulted the Ministry of Foreign Affairs in Kingstown for their assistance. They informed us that in order to secure the type of visa that we were requesting, we needed to undergo medical examinations, including x-rays and blood tests, and to obtain a police record—a document certifying that we had no criminal convictions. At the end of the exercise, we observed that the medical tests for the family, plus the cost of the Filipino visas, plus the cost of sending the passports to Washington D.C. to obtain those visas, were covered mostly by the "extra salary" that we had received along with our July advance. Amen?

The process of applying for the Filipino visas was a hassle and a literal race against time. But here too, God worked things out beautifully! I remember the whole family spending a couple of days in Kingstown, scurrying here and there, to the police headquarters, to the Ministry of Foreign Affairs, and to the medical lab, filling out forms, waiting, then going again. By the time we got back to Bequia, we were just so tired! The police records normally take several days to obtain; however, through prayer and contacts with the right people in certain administrative positions both on Bequia and in Kingstown, we were able to secure them in one day. Yes, in one day! We took our medical forms to the resident doctor on Bequia, who turned out to be a Filipino. He appeared quite pleased with the fact that we were going to his country and I suspect this influenced his decision to complete the forms absolutely free. As for the passports, we got them back from Washington D.C. a mere five days before our scheduled departure from Bequia. I can't help saying it over and over: God is so good!

While all of this was going on, we were trying to buy the most economical tickets to New York. We had learned much earlier that it was better to fly to Trinidad and then to New York, so that's what we were planning to do. The fares had been going up lately—against our hopes. Jackie's contact person in Trinidad was her former teacher and long-time friend, Miss Pamela John, now deceased; she kept checking but for several weeks the result was pretty much the same. On our end, we just kept praying that God would take care of things. Then Miss John came to spend a few vacation days with us and when she was leaving we gave her what we hoped would be enough money, based on the actual quoted prices.

Well, by now you can guess, can't you? You have seen the pattern. Here's what happened: by the time we were ready to leave, Miss John informed us that she had identified a travel agency which could give us amazingly low fares to New York on the now-defunct Pace Airlines, a name I had never heard of before. And instead of paying US$2600, we paid a mere US$1900, a whopping savings of US$700!!

Awesome God!

Since we could not fly directly from Bequia to Trinidad, our plan was to take the ferry to Kingstown, spend the night with friends, and fly to Trinidad the following day. That would increase travel costs by a few hundreds, and with all our calculations, I don't think we had factored it in. However, the St. Vincent to Trinidad leg of our journey was made more affordable by the fact that I had received a complimentary ticket from another now-defunct airline, Caribbean Star. You see, in my spare time I had penned a poem about the airline and submitted it to them. The marketing manager was so pleased with my little rhyme, most of which I no longer remember, that she had requested and obtained my permission to publish it in their staff magazine; in return, they had offered me a ticket to any of their destinations. So we ended up needing to buy only three tickets.

## *Bye Bye Bequia*

Well, it was soon time to leave Bequia, the cosy little island we had called home since January 2000. The parting was a very touching one. At worship that final Sabbath morning, the church gave us a fond farewell and a tangible financial token; we also received monetary gifts from several other members. My wife gave a heartfelt response but I was too emotional, so I put off my speech until the afternoon program. By then I was certainly more composed, and after listening to members of the church paying individual tribute, I started my farewell speech. It wasn't easy. I had to keep battling a lump in my throat. The only other time I came so close to tears in a church was when I was repeating my wedding vows ten years and fourteen days earlier.

We spent practically the whole of Sunday and most of Monday, down to the time of our departure, cleaning up our residence from one corner to the next. Our aim, as before, was to turn it over in a spotlessly clean condition; that was one way we felt we could express our gratitude to our benefactors. It was a busy but exciting couple of days. One elderly brother invited us over to his home for a farewell lunch that included so much pizza that we had to carry lots of extras home for dinner.

That Monday afternoon of July 28, 2003, my secretary and our dear friend, Mrs. Psyche Ollivierre, came with her taxi to drive us down to the pier—gratis. When we got there, we found a significant group of church folk waiting to see us off: the first elder, the women from Jackie's prayer group, some of my very close friends, some other senior brethren, and Brother and Sister Gooding, among others. It was really moving and again, I fought back the tears.

We crossed the ramp, paid our fares, and headed up the steps to the upper deck of the MV Admiral 1. Then at exactly 4:59, the blaring that I was so used to hearing from my porch sounded. The engines rumbled to life, churning water against the pier as we cast off. We glided past the water taxis, past the dozens of yachts moored nearby, and off toward the headland below the ruins of that ancient fort. From the deck I could see over to my far right the blue roof of Sister Gooding's villa and the white porch where time and again I had leaned over the railing to watch the ferries depart. I gazed nostalgically at the steep trail leading down to Princess Margaret

Beach from the house and scanned the entire beach for anyone still soaking up the last of the evening sunshine.

Soon, for the last time, we rounded the point, heading into the distance where the perennial placidity of the Caribbean Sea surrenders to the surges and swells of the Atlantic. I looked at Jackie and the children sitting quietly, the other passengers chatting or simply relaxing, the hills dropping steeply down into the dark blue-green sea, the water churning and seething in the ship's wake; I listened to the steady rhythmic rumble of the engine, the splash of the waves against the ship's starboard side, the whistling of the wind in my ears...

And I thought, "This is it. We are actually leaving."

Indeed, we had left, not knowing in one sense what lay out there but believing firmly on the other hand that God was in charge of whatever it would turn out to be.

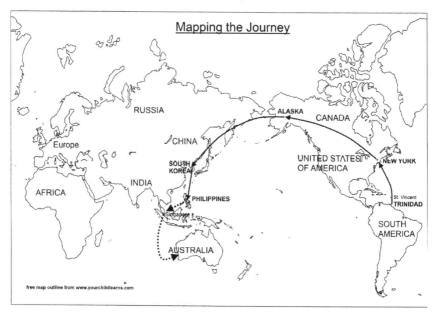

Map of the world showing our journey

# V

# Journey of Blessings

> *Now it happened one day that Elisha went to Shunem, where there was a notable woman, and she persuaded him to eat some food. So it was, as often as he passed by, he would turn in there to eat some food. And she said to her husband, "Look now, I know that this is a holy man of God, who passes by us regularly. Please, let us make a small upper room on the wall; and let us put a bed for him there, and a table and a chair and a lampstand; so it will be, whenever he comes to us, he can turn in there."*
> *And it happened one day that he came there, and he turned in to the upper room and lay down there. 2 Kings 4:8-11*

## *Prologue*

I steady my grip and lean forward, supporting myself against the chrome-plated upright pole as the morning rush-hour train screeches and grinds to a halt. I turn around to join the throng of commuters already pressing toward the exit door, knowing it's just a matter of seconds for the changeover before the public address system announces, "Stand clear of the closing doors, please." I shuffle forward, eyes on my sneakers, trying not to bump into the person ahead of me. I step cautiously across the platform gap onto the well-worn, dirty-looking concrete subway platform. I raise my eyes, spot a gap in the surging crowd, and charge toward it in a few long strides while scores of commuters hustle down the escalators and dash past, trying desperately to get into the train before the doors shut, as if that were the last train for the next twenty-four hours.

Eyes upward as if yearning for the light of open skies, I climb the moving stairs, half walking, half riding, emerging into the fresh crisp September morning air—a distinct contrast from the musty heat of the subway. I look left, then right, scanning for now-familiar landmarks and reading the traffic flow, just to ensure that I'm heading in the right direction.

Right! I must turn right... not left, as I did on the first day and almost got lost.

Dwarfed by towering skyscrapers I walk, past that rough-looking, cap-wearing, newspaper-selling man, past the dimly lit shop where that distinctive smell of brewing coffee mixed with cigar smoke comes from, past the grating where heat from the underground railway rises through the pavement, past the pedestrian detour around construction scaffolding, toward the next traffic lights. The crossing light is red, but as soon as I arrive, it turns green. I cross briskly, scores of other foot travellers following. One more block, a right turn, then about seventy-five steps and I'm there.

I climb the short flight of steps at the front of the building, open the heavy wooden door, and rest my lunch bag in a corner. Turning around, I head back down the steps toward a huge dumpster covered over with a blue tarpaulin which is tied securely all the way around. I start loosening the tie-down ropes, quickly working my way all around and finally pulling the tarp off toward the empty pavement, exposing the heap of rubble dumped unevenly inside. I fold the tarp, then take it through a narrow basement window into a courtyard below street level.

I return to the front lobby to retrieve my lunch bag lest someone helps himself to a free lunch; then I return to my basement corner and sit, waiting. The other guys are not here yet. I'm the early bird. They will arrive within the next twenty minutes: three Americans, among them a seventeen-year-old who complains about the high cost of his rent, one Jamaican, and one bloke from some Central American country which I no longer remember. The most senior guy will assign me my duties for the morning: I'll probably be carrying some more drywall up the narrow stairs like I did the day before, or working the pulley down to the basement to take some rubble out to the dumpster. And the senior guy will remind me, "Make sure that when the boss comes around he finds you doing something—anything!" And I'll be thinking, "Yeah, right! You slackers!"

But they haven't arrived yet, so I have time to sit, think and pray. I know it: I'll be tired before the end of this day. And I won't even get to see Jackie and the children this evening; I'm going to the Bronx.

And I ask myself, "What am I doing here? What on earth?"

I've gone from being the guy with the keys to the hired, unskilled labourer down at the work site, from the well-known to the virtually unknown. This is not the familiarity of Bense Church or comfort zone of Temple School. This is a long way from the tranquillity of my Bequia bedroom or even from the disciplinary challenges of the classroom and principal's office. This is New York, a place I've always wanted to see but never wanted to be; New York, a city described by singer Alicia Keys as the "concrete jungle where dreams are made;" New York, the scene of the September 11 terrorist attacks; New York, the last place in America where I would choose to settle—if I ever chose to live in America. Nothing about this place appeals to me, so what am I doing here?

I think you know the answer: I'm just passing through. Didn't come here to have my dreams made. Didn't come here to stay. In a few weeks, I'll be out of here. Gone! Goodbye, New York!

But for now, I've got to do this. I've got to work, to make a few badly-needed bucks!

Got to!

In my mind, I replay the departure from Bequia: that Monday afternoon when we left our friends on the pier, boarded the ferry and sailed around the point, "not knowing in one sense what lay out there but believing firmly on the other hand that God was in charge of whatever it would turn out to be." Remember?

Let's return there and pick up the story at that point, shall we?

## *Further Favours*

When we got to Kingstown, two of our friends were waiting for us at the pier. They helped us pack our bulging, overweight suitcases and bags into their car and drove us to their home. Although we knew that this would be our last time together in a long while, our hosts graciously allowed us to go to bed early, and after a restful night, they taxied us over to the airport in the morning.

There, an unexpected situation popped up. The check-in clerk at the Caribbean Star counter informed me that the only confirmed seat to Trinidad at 8:15 was mine; Jackie and the children were confirmed for the 7:05 p.m. flight. I tried to convince him that there must have been an error—that we had received confirmation for all bookings through the travel agency on Bequia, but that was to no avail. We had to accept the separation, the reality of Jackie spending the day in St. Vincent with two tired children, and the fact that she would not be able to see some of her friends in Trinidad as she had hoped to.

Thankfully, even though our host of the previous night had gone to his job, Miss Swift, a close friend who was also Annique's teacher, had stayed around and was therefore able to take them home for the entire day. Thankfully also, I was able to take the all of our luggage along with me, so they did not have to worry about that. Thus, even in the midst of this disappointment, we received a great blessing.

On arriving in Trinidad, it took a little negotiation and some prayer to get the luggage released to me, since they were not all tagged in my name. I explained that we were in transit to New York and that unexpectedly the others had been forced to wait for a later flight while I was given the care of the luggage. Once the customs officers had decided to let me have them, they cleared me through customs quite easily, sparing me the hassle of opening any of the many pieces that I was carrying.

Outside, I met Jackie's father with one of his neighbours waiting for us with a car. Imagine their surprise when I emerged alone. But there was someone else waiting for us: Mr. Junior Archer, a good friend from the sister island of Tobago and a former faculty member from our CUC days. He was standing there with the keys to a rented sport utility vehicle, not for himself but for us, so that we could drive ourselves around the following day and avoid the inconvenience of catching rides on public transportation. Honestly, I did not know how to react. I hardly knew what to say. I was so overwhelmed by his generosity. And all he wanted was simply to do his old friends a favour before they left for…only God knew how long. Wow!

After catching my breath, I quickly worked things out: my father-in-law would take our luggage home and I would drive around with Junior for the day, depending on where I needed to go. So I was able to visit "Dear Old CUC" and say goodbye to some close friends I met there that day. I was also able to go with Miss John to collect our tickets for New York.

Thus, when Jackie and the children arrived later that evening, Miss John, Junior and I were on hand to greet them. That night I drove my tired family home in the rented vehicle, and the next morning Jackie and I were able to drive over to her grandfather's home in the countryside to bid him goodbye.

As I think back on this experience, I thank God for sending Junior because I am sure we would not have been able to accomplish so much without the vehicle. It was truly a huge blessing.

## *Networking in New York*

Shortly after 3:00 p.m. on Wednesday July 30, 2003, we left Trinidad on our nearly five-hour flight to New York. En route, I sent up a simple prayer to God: "Lord, as a token or sign that you will be with us during our stay in New York, please let us have a smooth passage through Immigration when we get to John F. Kennedy Airport. I prayed thus because I knew that since September 11, 2001 (commonly referred to as 9/11), passing through Immigration at American ports of entry had become more stringent than it used to be. I also remained aware of the fact that, as stated earlier, we only had the means to reach New York and were depending on God to take us the rest of the way. I must confess that I was a bit nervous to see how that prayer would be answered.

Well, when we got to the immigration desk, things went so smoothly that you would think I was entering Dominica. Interestingly, the immigration officer did not address Jackie or me directly; he went straight for Christopher. Holding up a passport, he asked,

"Who is this?'

"That's me."

"And who is this?"

"That's my sister," Chris answered, pointing to Annique.

The officer showed him the two remaining passports and he identified them correctly. Then he asked him what his parents did (as a profession) and where we were going, to which the five-year-old boy again gave the right answers. I reckon if we had something to hide, we would have been caught because the child would have told the truth.

So with a smile and an air of satisfaction, we literally sailed through immigration. My prayer was answered. And watch this: we had visas valid for only three months... but the officer gave us permission to stay six months! That would turn out to be very important in the end, for whereas we had intended to leave New York on September 30, we had to remain some two weeks longer.

While waiting for Jackie's sister to pick us up, I just kept saying, "Praise the Lord" over and over. It's as if God had just given us the assurance that we would not end up stuck in New York indefinitely; He would work things out so that we could complete our journey to the Philippines.

Well, we spent the next ten days or so just resting at our temporary home in the borough of Queens. It was a quiet routine: sleeping late at night and getting out of bed late the next morning, simply relaxing, watching TV, having meals, doing light housework, or going to the nearby playground with the children.

During those first few days, I made contact with several of my old friends and told some of them that I was looking for a short-term job to help raise some extra cash. By putting it this way, I did not disclose the truth of our situation. I did not want them to know that we really did NOT yet have the money to purchase our tickets. A few of them promised to help but they advised me up front that I would most likely end up on a construction site. I couldn't imagine what that would look and feel like: me, leaving the classroom and office, lifting building materials on a construction site, working in a field where I had absolutely no experience. But I told them that it was fine; I had no problems with the idea. My attitude was, "Where there is a need, there is a will, and where there's a will, there's a way."

One of the friends I contacted was Sister Etheline Magloire, a woman who had served as the director of my church's Pathfinder Club during my late childhood. She was better known as the person who ran the biggest shop in the village back then, but otherwise she had been very influential in shaping the lives of many of the young children under her care in that Pathfinder club. In fact, saying it more correctly, it was Etheline who contacted me after hearing from my close friend and former CUC roommate, Lester Joseph, that I was in New York. Etheline invited me over to her apartment in The Bronx, the borough where she lived, on the second Sabbath afternoon of our stay. There, I was supposed to give a short presentation to a group gathered for a session of prayer and praise. She arranged for two other friends, Claude and Ketty, to pick me up.

When I got to Etheline's apartment that Sabbath afternoon, I had no idea what blessings were in store for me and my family over the next seven or eight weeks. It was a pretty sentimental reunion: Etheline welcomed me with an embrace that mothers reserve for their long-lost sons. We stood hugging each other at the door for almost a minute, interrupting the session already in progress, embracing, just taking in the moment. She was moved to tears, and I understood why; and when she explained to the other believers gathered there, they too understood why. We had not seen each other in over twenty years.

Before I left that evening, Etheline extended an invitation to the rest of my family to spend the following Sabbath with her. (She was actually disappointed that I had not brought them along with me.) I graciously accepted, so the next Friday evening, we left our temporary home in Queens and worked our way through the subway system to East 233rd Street. We spent a wonderful Sabbath with Etheline and her several friends who dropped by, including Lester, Claude, Ketty and Dee, old friends from Dominica. The next afternoon, Jackie and the kids returned home and I stayed over so that I could get to work early Monday morning.

This was the beginning of what I sometimes refer to as our Oasis. Indeed, we spent the next seven Sabbaths with Etheline who literally refreshed us. You see, it was challenging to meaningfully observe the Sabbath where we were staying in Queens; by contrast, Etheline's apartment afforded us the opportunity to have family worship, find time for prayer and study, go to church, and enjoy the company of friends who shared our faith. So we developed a pattern of leaving Queens on Friday afternoon, spending Sabbath with Etheline, and going back home on Sunday evening or sometimes on Monday morning.

I counted seven Sabbaths at "The Oasis." I thought that was pretty significant: seven sevens! A full week of Sabbaths! No wonder we were so blessed. We even had the opportunity, courtesy of Etheline, to attend a Camp Meeting of the North-Eastern Conference and to visit three or four churches in New York, including the one where she worships. I also had the privilege of ministering at two of these churches through singing, playing the piano, and preaching.

Another blessing that came through Etheline was meeting Roselia, another Bense native. Etheline arranged for us to go to Roseila's church in New Jersey one Sabbath. There we led out in the Sabbath School program and enjoyed wonderful fellowship with the small congregation. Roselia and her husband entertained us at their lovely countryside home and gave us VIP treatment by sending us back home in a shiny, jet-black limousine. I don't think any of us had ever been in a limo before, so that was something to savour!

That wasn't all. Etheline also took us to visit the home of Brother Cyrus and Sister Amy White, Dominicans residing in Brooklyn. That was very special to me because of the long-standing bond between the Whites and my family. As far as I can recall, my parents were good friends of that couple; that explains why two of my siblings, Corinthia and Figuhr, lived with the Whites for some time while they attended the Portsmouth Secondary School in the early seventies. And then there was my old primary school classmate and lifelong friend, Sheryl, one of the four daughters of that family. So visiting the Whites was something truly sentimental. I fondly remember sitting at the piano that Sabbath afternoon, singing some old-time hymns and favourite songs I had learned from my father and reminiscing on the "good old days."

But let me return to the part-time work I did in New York, something in which I also saw God's hand of blessing. Etheline helped me secure a job with a brother at her church, Brother Willie. He was a floor maintenance specialist, and for two or three days a week I went with him and his crew to a house under construction to complete the preparation of the wooden floor, or to a home where the floor needed a complete makeover, or one where the owners probably just needed some carpet cleaning or polishing. It was hard work, but I learned the value of each man's trade. Willie did a fantastic job, and he directed me as if I had arrived to stay and therefore needed to learn the skills of my new trade really fast. One day, as he watched me lifting his heavy equipment into and out of his work van, he joked that by the end of my stint with him my biceps would look like those of Popeye the Sailor Man. And yeah; Willie also paid me quite well.

During those days, Etheline let me stay at her apartment so I could get to and from Brother Willie's home in Mamaroneck without having to commute to Queens and back, which would cost me several hours. She faithfully prepared and packed a warm meal, complete with dessert and snack in between, so that I would not have to overly burden myself with cooking or buying food. On the days when she was home, she packed so much into my lunch bag that my workmates couldn't help commenting on the amount of food that I ate at lunchtime. Etheline even took care of my laundry. In short, she mothered me. And on weekends she still mothered my family!

My old buddy Lester made it easy for me to get to work at 6:45 on mornings by picking me up at Etheline's apartment and dropping me off at Willie's, which was less than five minutes from his place of work at the Bank of New York offices in Mamaroneck. Some evenings he would also take me around to visit friends, to eat or to shop before dropping me back at the apartment.

But shortly before we were due to leave, we learned that we had to spend an extra two weeks in New York, and after reassessing my situation with Etheline I decided to switch to another job. This time I worked five days a week for three weeks with another Adventist contractor on a project on East 24th Street in Manhattan. It was a totally different, often more strenuous experience, but I was happy to work five days a week which entitled me to take home quite a lot more money. There was only one other professing Christian on the project, so I tried to share my faith with a couple of the guys and gave Spanish-language tracts to the worker from Central America. I still had the opportunity to stay at Etheline's apartment if I wished, so I alternated between there and our home in Queens.

Every time I look back on the New York experience, I thank God for blessing my family and me through the people we knew and with whom we were able to connect. I have talked much about the role that Etheline played, and that's something I could never talk too much about. I also mentioned Roselia, but there were several significant others. Lester was right there for us. Not only did he help me get to and from work, but he also drove me around as much as he could to reconnect with some of our old friends. Lester took me to Boston one Sabbath, invited me to play at his church, and organized a Sunday morning breakfast-lunch for my family at his brother Benjie's home and a Sunday evening barbecue at the home of Eric Gordon, my neighbour from childhood days. He also bought treats for my kids and took my family out to dinner one evening. Despite his busy life, this man just made himself available to us, something for which we remain truly thankful. Without him, things wouldn't have been the same.

Then there was Ketty, who grew up right next to Bourne School, my friend from primary and secondary school days. Ketty linked up with us from the second Sabbath when we attended her church, the Queensboro Temple in Queens. The next Sabbath she took us home for lunch and the following Sabbath, when I went to Boston, she took my family under her wings. For several Sabbaths thereafter, Ketty was there, taking us to places of worship where Etheline wanted to go. Sometimes it seems that Ketty had other plans of her own but she just shelved them so she could be there for us. Such unselfish love!

There was also Claude, a witty, well-built, well-read, former secondary schoolmate and friend who was described by his peers as being usually difficult to reach but who certainly made his presence felt during our stay. Claude was the first person who took me over to Etheline's house. He often stopped by Etheline's and, being a close associate of both Ketty and Etheline, sometimes accompanied us on our outings. On a couple of occasions, he took the family back to Queens at the end of our Oasis stop. He really helped make us feel at home. One evening, Claude handed me a few hundred-dollar notes from his wallet and told me with a smile, "That is just a small token. It is not the real thing yet." I was at a loss for words.

We met many new faces courtesy of Etheline and the others—faces like kindhearted Brother and Sister Brooke, Brother and Sister Hunte of St. Maarten, Sister Jane Austrie from Dominica, Sisters Loban and Robinson from the Mamaroneck church, and others too numerous to mention. These wonderful people were simply pleased with what they had heard about us so they wholeheartedly endorsed our plan. Some questioned why we had chosen to go so far from home, but on hearing our explanation they offered their words of encouragement and support. Just as He had done before, God spoke to me through His people, confirming that this was really His call.

But for all its worth, our stay in New York would not have been possible were it not for the kindness of Jackie's sister, Angela, and her husband, Hollis. For several reasons, this was the foundation for all the other blessings we received in New York. First, we could not have stayed at our Bequia location any longer, neither could we have moved to another place, since a double stop would have cost us much more. Next, registration at AIIAS was not until the middle of October. Finally, our last pay check was for the month of August. What could we have done between those times? It was so much easier to stay in New York for a while before proceeding to the Philippines. So the Lewis's decision to accommodate an entire family at their home with their own family for two long months (turned out to be ten weeks) was really decisive. It was the tremendous blessing that I dare not fail to mention. I cannot begin to imagine how things might have turned out if they had not been there for us.

## *Delayed Departure; Bountiful Blessings*

September 29 had been set as the date of our departure from New York. I had been working for several weeks, but somehow the money did not accumulate as much as we were hoping. Jackie had been purchasing some of the items she was sure we would need in the Philippines because we did not have a fair idea of the cost of living over there. What's more, we thought it prudent to contribute to the budget of the family that was hosting us for such an extended period. Of course, there was our regular weekend commute to "The Oasis" and back. All in all, time was running out and our money was still way below the target figure.

Speaking of a target figure, I had been praying for several days that the Lord would help us find at least six thousand dollars to cover our airfares, registration fees, and the cost of setting up our new home in the Philippines. After what God had done for us in Bequia, I did not put it beyond Him at all, so to speak, for I remembered the Lord asking in Jeremiah 32:27, "Is there anything too hard for Me?"

So there you have it: we were roughly two weeks away from departure and we still did not have the money we needed. That was enough to raise our anxiety levels to breaking point. I remember talking the situation over with Jackie when she looked quite uneasy; she was sure that God would work something out, but the experience of waiting was just so tense! I knew how it felt. At one stage while we were talking, I felt the same headache that I had felt that morning in January when we discovered that we had to send our deposits to AIIAS sooner than we thought. Somehow I was able to fight off that headache, but trust me: it was like suspense in a movie.

One thing we were sure of: we did not want to get stuck in New York. Some friends had suggested that we remain there longer or even stay for good, but both Jackie and I were totally opposed to the idea. Sometimes the ugly thought came up: "What if we don't get through?" It would be so embarrassing to see our bold plans failing, wouldn't it? Those were the seeds of doubt that the enemy was trying to sow in our minds, but we had to fight them with the weapons of prayer and faith in God's promises.

Indeed, we could do nothing but strengthen ourselves in the Lord and wait. So pray we did. And wait we did. I used to get up in the wee hours of the morning and just talk to God about the matter. When I arrived at work, I would find a little secluded spot in the basement of the building and pray before starting my duties. At break time, I would pray again, and again at lunchtime and just before leaving for home. I remember calling the children into the bedroom on several occasions to pray, explaining beforehand what we were going to pray for and why. We wanted the experience to be a lesson of faith for them, so we all prayed, they in their simple way, that God would send us the money. We admitted to them that we did not know where it would come from but we believed that the Lord would provide.

Then about ten days before our scheduled departure, we got an urgent message from Dr. Mulzac telling us that we should not leave New York until we heard from him. Believe me, that was not what we wanted to hear. But by the next day or two he sent us word again, this time telling us that because of changes in the AIIAS calendar, it would not be convenient for us to travel on the dates that we planned. In brief, based on his message, we had to spend two more weeks in New York. It was disappointing because we were really looking forward to leaving, but that delay proved to be for the best, for it was then that the Lord fulfilled His promise.

After assessing the information we had received, we changed our date of departure to October 15; this would get us to AIIAS on October 17 and allow us about a week and a half to settle in before the start of school. Meanwhile, Jackie kept trying to find the cheapest airfares to the Philippines. Her persistence paid off when she came across a travel agency run by a Filipino man on the west side of lower Manhattan. By all indications, his price was really good; it was the best we had heard of since we began researching airfares back there on Bequia.

But we still did not have the money.

One day I decided to go to Etheline's apartment, instead of our abode in Queens, so I could enjoy a more peaceful atmosphere in which to complete the sermon I planned to preach that upcoming Sabbath. I think it was a Tuesday. When I went there that evening I called Jackie to find out how they were doing and learned from her that on Etheline's suggestion, she had worked out another business plan which rested solely on the belief that God would answer our prayer. We would borrow two thousand dollars from her sister Angela with a promise to pay it back by the following Monday. That sounded a bit crazy but I agreed. You see, I just believed God would do something to make it happen, so that night, instead of asking Him to make it happen, I simply thanked Him for what He was about to do.

The next day I prayed at my usual times, and when I returned to Queens I told Jackie that I was going to contact a few other friends to see if they could help. So I went to the computer down in the basement room and typed a letter that started something like this:

"Hi …(person's Name), Do you have any rich friends? I don't mean Bill Gates rich, or Oprah rich, but rich enough to be very comfortable. You see, I need to raise two thousand dollars by next Monday; that's in connection with our going to the Philippines."

The rest of the letter, which was quite short and to the point, asked the recipient very tactfully to discuss my little project with one or two more of their "rich friends" and see what they could come up with. I also included my phone number since time was of the essence.

When I finished typing the letter, I placed my hand on the computer's monitor and prayed, asking God that He would answer my prayer by letting at least one recipient respond favourably. I sent the letter to only three very special friends out of the one-hundred-and-twenty-plus people in my Hotmail address book: one in South Lancaster (Massachusetts, USA), the second in Trinidad, and the third in the state of Texas. That was Wednesday.

On Thursday evening I was relaxing at home after work when the phone rang and someone told me the call was mine. On the other end of the line was Avonda, the friend from Texas. The conversation went something like this:

"Hello! Erickson speaking."

"Hi, Erickson; this is Avonda."

"Hey, Avonda! Good to hear you. How're you doing?"

"I'm good. How was your day?"

"It's been good. Just got back from work and just chilling."

"Ok. Well, I got your email and I just thought I'd chip in. I want to send you half of that amount."

"What? Are you serious? Say that again."

"I said..., I... want... to... send... you... half... of... that... amount!"

"What! Oh my... ! I don't know what to say. Thank you so much! Thank you!"

"That's okay. How would you like me to send it?"

I quickly gave her Angie's name and address since Angie was the one we needed to pay back, and she promised that the check would be at my doorstep the following day. We must have chit-chatted a bit longer before we hung up, but I was just blown away by her generosity.

Sure enough, while I was away at work, a check for $1000 was delivered to Angie's doorstep! Jackie collected it and had the pleasure of handing it over to Angie, whose face betrayed the question on her mind, "Where did you get this?" But that was just step one.

That Sabbath, I preached at Mamaroneck, Etheline's church. Jackie, Ketty and I assisted Etheline with her Sabbath School program, and I played the piano, sang, and preached the mid-morning sermon. At the potluck lunch we met a whole lot of people, many of whom were thrilled to hear of our mission. In the mid-afternoon Jackie and the kids stayed over at Ketty's apartment while I went to the Co-op City Church for the afternoon program. Later, Ketty picked me up and we all headed to Etheline's apartment where we were supposed to attend a prayer and praise meeting.

When we got there, which was over an hour behind schedule, we met a small group assembled. There was Lester, Roselia and her family, her mother, and a lady whom we had met earlier that morning at Mamaroneck. Within the hour, still others came until the little living room could hardly accommodate anyone else. Etheline led out in a meaningful, encouraging session of praise, testimony and prayer.

To my pleasant surprise, after the final prayer, Etheline invited those who had brought their gifts to drop them in a basket on the centre table. What do you suppose? From all corners of the room came many different sizes and colours of envelopes, dropping into a neat little pile in the basket. When the last one was dropped, Etheline handed me the basket with instructions to go and count the money in the bedroom. Jackie and I went and we started counting. By the time we were through, we had about one thousand six hundred dollars in cash and about four hundred in pledges. Jackie then whispered to me that Roselia had promised to make up the difference between whatever we counted and two thousand dollars—in spite of having made her own contribution already. So when we announced the final tally, Roselia left the apartment, walked to the nearest ATM, and returned with the difference. So that night we actually got the full two thousand in cold cash with an understanding that the pledges were to be fulfilled later. Blown away, one more time!

But there was more to come. The following night, Claude called in at Etheline's apartment to see me. He did not even come in; he just stood at the door and chatted with me briefly. At the end of our conversation he handed me an envelope—his contribution. When I opened it, I could not believe my eyes. There was one thousand dollars in cash! For a moment I was speechless. I simply did not have the words to thank either Claude or God. Blown away—the third time!

That night, we shared with the children what God had done and we each prayed a prayer of thanksgiving. He had not only sent us two thousand dollars; we had gotten over four thousand between Friday and Sunday night. Praise the Lord!

Before we left New York, we received another seven to eight hundred dollars in gifts. In retrospect, I believe God was trying to show us that He knew our precise needs. I believe He was blessing us openly for exercising faith and borrowing two thousand dollars on the belief that He would supply the funds to pay it back.

Imagine our joy when we handed Angie the remaining one thousand that Monday afternoon. Imagine her surprise too. But the success of this faith venture left me with one important lesson: once you enter into partnership with God, you can never fail because He NEVER fails.

**ERICKSON FABIEN**

## *Passage to the Philippines*

We left Etheline's apartment that Sunday evening with mixed emotions. We knew we were not going to see her again before our departure, so all the goodbyes were said then. It was really touching. She had become such a part of our lives in such a short space of time.

For the next few days I stayed in Queens, opting not to go back to work. I took some time to relax and help with the shopping and packing. I decided that on the Tuesday I would head back to Mamaroneck to say goodbye to Brother Willie and my first workmates; so I slept over at Etheline's for the last time and took the early train to Mamaroneck, arriving there just at the time when we normally left for work. They were surprised and pleased to see me, and since one of the guys had called to say he was sick, Brother Willie asked me to go to work with them that morning. I was not prepared, but I gave in and went to work up till about 11:30, making some additional change in the process.

That evening Ketty stopped by for the last time. She had been tremendously good to us, and we really appreciated that final visit.

Wednesday October 15 was a long day. We spent it at home, trying to stuff the last ends into the already overstuffed suitcases: we sat on them, jumped on them, rolled them, slapped them, trying not to leave anything behind. There were at least eight pieces, besides hand luggage. Afternoon finally came; then the evening rolled into the night—the night of departure. We were finally on our way!

Bundling everything into Hollis's people mover van, we drove over to John F. Kennedy Airport where we encountered a little scare: our flight reservation was declared "not confirmed!" At least, that's what the check-in clerk said. Yes, it was a little scary as all kinds of thoughts raced through my mind, but we were confident that this would be sorted out. Provisionally, I had secured from the ticket agent the exact reference number of our reservation, so when the check-in clerk came a second time with the news that we were not confirmed, I passed her the number and she was able to trace the problem—a bad spelling of our names. Phew! Relief! Problem solved! We were checked in, boarded a few minutes later, and were airborne shortly after midnight.

About two minutes into the flight, I turned to my left and looked at Christopher, Annique and Jackie (they sat in that order). I gave Jackie a short whistle to get her attention and gave her a thumbs-up signal. She got the message: we are on our way!

Yes! Amen!

Hallelujah!

Thank you Jesus!

I felt that familiar lump returning to my throat, undoubtedly from the realization that God had done so much for us in bringing us through. I fought back the urge to cry; I just prayed another prayer of thanks to God and tried to settle down for the long flight.

It was some six hours before we touched down in Anchorage, Alaska, for refuelling. We had to get off the plane, of course, and wait for the greater part of an hour. Then we boarded again for the long haul to Incheon airport in South Korea.

That leg was just a little over eight hours long, but it seemed like an endless night because we were flying westward. In fact, it was the longest night of my life. We arrived there some time between six and seven that morning—not Thursday, but Friday morning. After a couple of hours waiting, we started the final segment of our journey to Manila, which took just under four hours. We got into Manila, a tired but thankful quartet, shortly before midday on Friday October 17, 2003. The whole journey had taken us some 24 hours.

…..

It was a bit of an uneasy walk out of the plane, not because we were tired but because we knew that we could encounter some difficulty at the airport's immigration desk. In fact, Dr. Mulzac had warned us that an African student had recently been put on a flight and sent home. As such, he had even suggested we make an onward reservation to some other destination, like Hong Kong, just to be safe. In the very least, we needed to be sure we had a valid return ticket. Well, we knew that our papers were in order: we had the right kind of visa and valid return tickets, plus my acceptance letter and our letters of invitation from AIIAS. So armed with these and with a prayer, we walked up to the immigration desk where we were last in line.

Mysteriously, just before we reached the desk, a second officer came and stood right beside the one who was on duty. When I handed in my documents, he took the letter, read it, looked at us and told the first man to let us through.

Can you see what we saw? We saw in that little scene the providence of God. It seemed as if the Lord just sent that second man there so that we would not encounter any problems. What can I say but "Praise the Lord?"

We followed the directions we had received and soon emerged into the arrival area. The sweltering heat announced it: we were back in the tropics—in Manila, to be more precise. I had to tear off the coat that had been my comfort for the past twenty-four hours. In a few moments we saw Dr. Mulzac, who had just arrived. We were all so delighted to see him!

The Mulzac family back in the day

## *AIIAS Arrival*

After the hugs and welcomes, we packed our bulging suitcases into an AIIAS van and drove straight to the campus; that is, as straight as the snail-paced traffic could permit. I kept thinking all along, "Here we are at last!" And as we drove through the AIIAS gates, I felt an overwhelming wave of emotions. This was it! We had made it! That iconic administration building, that welcoming Bell Tower, those well-manicured lawns and ubiquitous coconut palms: they were no longer merely in the realm of photography. This was reality! We were actually at AIIAS!

Our initial excitement was tempered by the fact that we did not have an apartment on the campus to go to. (Just before leaving New York, we had received word from the Office of Student Services that they had no apartment ready for us and were therefore asking our permission to seek off-campus housing. We had no choice. Neither did they, since we had applied for and paid our housing deposit.) So Dr. Mulzac took us directly to his residence where we bundled our suitcases and bags into the room they had prepared for us. Almost immediately Jackie and I went with someone from Student Services to look at a house in a nearby district of the municipality of Silang. It proved to be pretty near the campus but we did not like it, so Dr. Mulzac invited us to stay at his home until Student Services helped us find a better one, and that's where we remained for the rest of October.

It was graduation weekend when we arrived. I remember having a meal, catching a shower, and ...yes, going to bed somewhere between four and five that afternoon. (Crazy!) I was awakened a few hours later by the noises of people walking and talking in the house, and I kept thinking, "Why are they being so noisy? Don't they have any idea what time it is?" whereas I was the one who had completely lost track of time. Jetlag! I had always heard about it but now I was experiencing it first-hand.

The next day, we were still too tired and disoriented to even think of getting out of bed and going to church, which started at eight. It wasn't until later that Sabbath afternoon that Jackie and I took our first walk around the campus that would later become our home for many months.

The Mulzac family took excellent care of us for those first two and a half weeks. They waited patiently while we struggled to overcome our crazy sleep-and-wake patterns and ensured that we were well fed. Fortunately, we had arrived at a time when school was out for a short break, so we had sufficient time to relax, unwind and become oriented. After a few days, the children and I got registered for school, and about a week later, Student Services succeeded with securing another apartment for us. This one was just about two minutes by car from the campus gate. Again, with the Mulzacs' help, we were able to shop for our household needs and on November 1, we moved in. We were on our own again, starting a new life.

The Bell Tower and Administration Building at AIIAS

# VI

# THE PHILIPPINE EXPERIENCE

> *So he went and did according to the word of the Lord, for he went and stayed by the Brook Cherith, which flows into the Jordan. The ravens brought him bread and meat in the morning, and bread and meat in the evening; and he drank from the brook. And it happened after a while that the brook dried up, because there had been no rain in the land.*
>
> *Then the word of the Lord came to him, saying, "Arise, go to Zarephath, which belongs to Sidon, and dwell there. See, I have commanded a widow there to provide for you... The bin of flour was not used up, nor did the jar of oil run dry, according to the word of the Lord which He spoke by Elijah." 1Kings 17:5-9, 16.*

## *Prologue*

We're standing outside the heavy white metal gates, talking in small groups, waiting to be admitted. We have just arrived, prayed, and been briefed on the day's program by Dr. Paoring Ragui, Vice-President for Student Services at AIIAS as well as Pastor Lee Myun Ju, a doctoral student from South Korea. A sign above the gate, beneath rows of barbed wire stretching from one side to the next, reads, "Bureau of Jail Management and Penology, Dasmariñas Municipal Jail, Dasmariñas, Cavite." They know we're coming, as we do every Saturday morning, so we don't expect to be standing here long.

Soon, were hear clanking. Keys are being turned. The left side of the gate swings open revealing the stern faces of two security guards, including the one who has opened the gate. The other security officer has a rubber stamp and stamp pad in his hands. He beckons us forward and, one by one, we pause long enough for him to print something on our right hand. It's always our right hand. If we extend the left one, he motions for us to extend the right one. I joke with one of my friends about this insistence, connecting it to the mark of the beast found in the book of Revelation; the guard looks at me but says nothing.

We're all clear. Everyone traverses the paved grey exercise zone cum basketball court and heads for the entrance to the covered assembly area, which is at the far right of the court. Inmates are calling through the bars atop their cell walls, whistling, trying to get our attention, especially that of the women in our group. We ignore them as well as those carrying out their duties in the buildings and spaces nearby.

We enter the assembly area which, except for a few rough wooden seats and a couple of tables, is more like a bare, open hall. To the far left is a toilet (known in the Philippines as a "Comfort Room" or "CR"). To my right is a narrow corridor or passage from which will emerge scores of prisoners once they have been given the all clear to come out.

We don't have long to wait. Here they come—a stream... no, a throng of yellow tee-shirts and cropped heads. They make a beeline for the seat of their choice, most chattering excitedly, but some looking silent, sombre and even sinister; and when all the seats are taken the others just stand. They don't care if they sit or stand; they just want to be there. Some greet us with "Happy Sabbath;" others say *"Maligayang Araw ng Sabado"* (Tagalog for "Happy Sabbath Day"). We shake hands... we dare shake hands with those who extend a hand—dare, because many of the inmates seem to be afflicted with some contagious skin ailment.

Soon, everyone is settled and the session gets under way. The inmates, especially the new ones, are welcomed. *"Bago! Bago!"* ("New") a few of the regular ones shout; in response, the new ones stand briefly. We begin a rousing session of singing action choruses, including top-of-the-chart "Walk, walk, walk, in the light." I'm playing the keyboard, singing at the top of my voice and totally enjoying the sight of a room full of yellow tee-shirts moving one way and then the next, demonstrating with all the energy they can muster how we should walk in the light of God.

The singing gives way to a Bible study conducted by one of our team members. He usually goes for at least forty minutes, but this morning he's keeping it brief because there's a lot happening. We're having a baptism.

On the left between the entrance to the corridor and the CR are three barrels filled with water. At the appointed time, three pastors including Dr. Ragui and Pastor Lee, step forward and stand beside the barrels. The inmates, seventy of them, form three lines in the direction of those barrels. When each prisoner gets there, he ascends a single step, climbs over the edge, and sinks midriff-high into the water. The pastors raise one hand and after one of them pronounces a little speech, they lower their hand onto the head of the inmates, pushing them gently down into a crouched position in the barrel. The inmates rise, smiling, and embrace the pastor before climbing out of the barrel, while the rest of the prison ministry team continues singing until the next three inmates are in place. This is repeated until seventy inmates are baptised.

At the end, Dr. Ragui makes an appeal, inviting any inmate who may wish to be baptised to come forward. Nine new inmates respond and are baptised immediately. The group members are ecstatic: seventy-nine precious souls have taken their stand for Jesus today! Hallelujah!

We close the service and after congratulating the newly baptised men, pack our belongings and head for the exit. The gate is unlocked and swung open and we file through, gathering in a neat circle outside the gate for a debriefing session and prayer. Finally we bundle into our vans for the approximately twenty-five minute ride back to AIIAS.

About 1.2 kilometers from the campus gate, the van stops and I get off. I walk about eighty meters and arrive alongside a white metal gate, which I push open and walk through. My knock on the door is answered by my son, who is more than happy to have me back home.

Home! Yes, the new place we call home: a rented apartment in Silang, a town in Cavite State located some forty-five kilometres south of Manila.

The apartment in Silang where we first lived

## *Faith for Failing Finances*

We spent our first five Philippine months in that rented Silang apartment, commuting and sometimes walking to and from the campus. Our landlord was a very kind man who owned a few other properties in Silang and he did everything he could to make us, total strangers, comfortable. The Mulzacs continued providing strong support: whenever we needed help with anything, they were there, and they often came driving by just to make sure we were ok.

We also found new friends in the family of Carlton and Wanda Forbes, a Jamaican-American couple who had served in South Korea and had arrived at AIIAS a few weeks earlier. They moved into the upstairs portion of our rented building and as such became our close neighbours. Carlton owned a car, which proved to be a huge difference in our ability to get to school on mornings.

Being in that apartment was sometimes lonely but it gave us the time and space we needed to settle as a close-knit family once more. That's a privilege we had not enjoyed since leaving Bequia many weeks earlier, and it prepared us for the campus experience where children tended to have much more liberty.

I quickly got settled into the routine of student life again; that included rising early on mornings to study or complete assignments and staying late on the campus some evenings to be at the library. The children also got into their own stride at their respective schools, at least for a while: Christopher in the campus pre-school and Annique at the elementary school. My wife, meanwhile, remained at home, ensuring that when the children came home in the afternoon they were attended to, since my classes met mostly on afternoons.

Most Friday evenings we would head to the campus for sundown worship and take a ride back with the Mulzacs or the Forbes. On Sabbaths, we were back on campus, but as soon as we got there, we parted ways: Jackie and the children went to the main worship service followed by Sabbath School, while I, having joined the Prison Ministries, went along with the team to the Dasmariñas jail.

While all of this was happening, our meager balance at the Philippine National Bank was being steadily depleted with no immediate prospect of a reliable income to stop the decline. Things were just beginning to look a little more challenging when my wife landed a part-time editorial stint with the seminary journal. Around that time, too, almost out of the blue, I received a financial gift from a friend in New York who had missed the opportunity to give us her love gift while we were there. Those were the early drops of the showers of blessing which were to follow, but first, God allowed us to experience the dread of drought in order that we would appreciate more deeply his miraculous power and readiness to rain blessings on us.

It was early in February of 2004. By then, we had closed our account at the bank to avoid the penalty imposed on accounts that fell below the minimum balance, and we were living on whatever remained in our hands. One Monday, when Jackie and I counted our pesos, we realized that we were down to a mere ₱300, which at that time was worth just about US$6.00. That's down from the $6000 we had gathered in New York! All we had in the kitchen was some oats, some potatoes, some salt, a few onions, some oil, and possibly one or two other items, but certainly not much to go on. The cooking gas was almost done; in fact, we expected it to run out at any moment, so our plan was to save the 300 pesos to buy the gas and leave the rest to God.

As expected, the gas finished the following day, Tuesday, while Jackie was preparing a meal. I quickly picked up the tank, walked to the nearest dealer's, and bought a full one, returning home with only 3 pesos in change!

That was it!

We had hit the bottom of the bucket!

Let me dwell on this a little because I want it to sink in. Here we were, in some far-off land: my wife, I, and our two young children, with no money left! For the first time in our adult lives, we were both literally broke! Do you have any idea how that felt? But let me hasten to add, dear reader, that although we were broke, we were not broken. We were financially helpless but not hopeless. In one sense, we had reached the end; in another sense, this was just the beginning. For it is when we are at our lowest that God has the greatest opportunity to manifest his power.

The Almighty had arranged that just the week before, a Korean woman who was vacationing at the nearby Southern Asia Pacific Division headquarters had been seeking the services of an English tutor, and one of her friends who knew me had recommended me to her. Having held discussions with her and agreeing on my tuition fees, I started tutoring her two sons that very Wednesday, the day AFTER our money ran out! The next evening, which was Thursday, I walked home with 1200 pesos in my pocket—enough to buy food and a few other basic necessities for the next week.

Two weeks later, another Korean parent called me up and requested that I tutor two other young students at the same rate. It seemed that word had somehow gone around that I was doing a good job. Because of my afternoon engagements, we scheduled these new classes for Friday mornings. So for the next several weeks, I took home ₱1200 on Thursday afternoons and another ₱1200 on Friday mornings. Things were beginning to look better, won't you say?

By the time that first parent left for Korea, she had put me in touch with yet another family for tutoring, and when these left, they put me in touch with other families. And that's how it went on, month after month, for the two and a half years of my stay at AIIAS. At one point, I taught English for four consecutive hours after school. It was admittedly quite tiring, but it was just what I needed to do to keep the family's economy recovering from the recession into which it had fallen. Like the widow's oil in Elijah's days, the requests for tutoring never dried up; in fact, they were so many that I had to turn down some of them. God once more proved his faithfulness; He provided well beyond my simple expectations.

In the second half of February 2004, the Office of Student Services informed us that we had been assigned an apartment on the campus. That was really good news, believe me. It meant no more trudging up and down the back roads to avoid walking along the highway, no more catching jeepney rides to get to and from school or church. It also meant that finally we could feel more a part of the campus family and be able to enjoy all the activities that went on there. We could hardly wait.

And so it was that on March 31, 2004, we moved into student apartment F7. It felt like we had finally completed the last leg of our long journey.

I guess this could have been the end of our story of miracles if the Lord had chosen to let it happen that way, but it turned out that He had many other plans for us. We didn't know but He knew. We simply had to learn to walk with Him by faith, step by step, trusting in the promise He made many centuries ago through the prophet Jeremiah: "For I know the plans I have for you ...plans to prosper you and not to harm you, plans to give you hope and a future. Then you will call upon me and come and pray to me, and I will listen to you. You will seek me and find me when you seek me with all your heart" (Jeremiah 29:11-13, NIV). And as we walked, He just continued to come through for us over and over again.

By now you might have realized that the biggest challenge we faced on this whole journey was a financial one. We left home on a faith ticket, so to speak. We did not have the funds to see us through, neither did we know, at any step of the way, where they would come from. So, much of the trust that we had to exercise in God was related to His readiness to provide for us, in cash or in kind, that which we lacked.

I'm saying this because I don't want to leave anyone with the impression that trusting God is all about money, money, and more money. God knows exactly what our needs are at any point in our lives. Sometimes we have emotional needs, and at other times we have spiritual ones, just to mention a couple. The wonderful thing is that whatever those needs may be, we can be certain that God has already devised the very best means and is quite ready to implement them so as to ensure our happiness.

The seminary building          My family at AIIAS, 2004

Having said that, let me just share with you a few more examples of God's providence.

Despite my weekly earnings from English instruction, it was clear that we were not going to be able to pay all our bills: the monthly rent, the children's tuition, our own tuition, books, other fees, medical expenses, and the occasional student visa renewal fee, all of which added up to a huge mountain, sometimes more than a hundred thousand pesos high.

One day, I went to class with a burden on my mind. I needed 10,000 pesos to cover the cost of renewing our visas, and believe me, I didn't even have 10% of that. As we sat in Hebrew Grammar class that morning, Dr. Mulzac led us in a customary prayer session before actual instruction got under way. We split into several groups and in my group there were four of us: Dr. Mulzac himself, a well-to-do retired Korean businessman whom I would later know as Mr. Yang, another seminary student from Thailand, and me. As we knelt, Dr. Mulzac asked whether we had any specific prayer requests. I don't remember what Mr. Yang said, but the Thai student asked for a blessing on his pregnant wife, and I said I needed a financial blessing. That was it. We prayed, got up, and went on with the class.

Later that afternoon, Dr. Mulzac called me over to his office. When I got there he said, "Erickson, I believe God has answered your prayer. This man from Tagaytay City has been owing me 10,000 pesos for quite a long time now, and surprisingly, he just showed up today and handed it to me. I want you to have it." Unbelievable? But true! I was honestly at a loss for words. So the visas were paid for.

The next day, I was at our apartment when I received a telephone call. When I answered, a male voice asked,

"Is this Erickson Fabien's apartment?"

"Yes, it is," I confirmed.

"Thank you," the mystery caller said and then hung up.

About five minutes later, a student from mainland China showed up at my door with a fat-looking white envelope on which was inscribed my name. He handed it to me courteously and disappeared down the stairs just as swiftly as he had appeared, barely pausing long enough to hear my expressions of gratitude for whatever was in there. My first reaction was to call Jackie and the children into the bedroom. We closed the door excitedly and uttered a rather nervous prayer of thanks to God for...whatever and for whoever had sent it. Then we counted the money: another 10,000 pesos!!

Talk about a double portion of blessing! That was rent money for the month with some extra.

Isn't God good?

The financial blessings didn't stop there. One fine day near the end of October 2004, my wife told me that Mr. Yang had approached her about giving English lessons to a woman from mainland China who was more commonly addressed by her adopted English name, Ruth. Yang wanted to help both parties: Ruth, who was struggling with her classes because the challenges of the English language, and Jackie, who needed to earn some extra income to take care of those monthly bills, so he offered to pay her at a rate far superior to that which English tutors usually earned.

Now Jackie had never felt comfortable assuming the role of English teacher. For her, speaking and writing English was one thing; teaching it to speakers of other languages was a completely different ball game—which it is. But she took the job, and after conducting a few sessions she handed it over to me, despite my already heavy tuition load. I also gave English lessons to Ruth's daughter.

Well, at the end of my first month of tutoring, Mr. Yang sent me a fat white envelope, just as fat and as white as the first one I had received earlier, because it contained the identical amount. That explained where the first one had come from. After all, he had been there with me in that little prayer group in the Hebrew Grammar class!

Jackie and I set aside the Lord's tithe along with a freewill offering, and what remained, believe me, was just enough for the month's rent. Mr. Yang continued to send a fat white envelope faithfully and punctually for the next fifteen months, even after my tuition arrangement with Ruth and her daughter ended. Thus, from November 2004 to January 2006, I was able to pay my rent on time! And by the time those fat white envelopes stopped coming, we were just two months away from my graduation and had saved enough to see me through those two months.

Meanwhile, our good friend Roselia from New York had made us an offer to assist with the children's school fees, and after some consideration we accepted it. So every new term, as soon as we notified her, Roselia would send those fees and throw in something extra so the children could enjoy a few additional treats. We will always be thankful to God for her kindness and generosity.

Finally, from time to time we received, almost out of the blue, a love gift from someone somewhere: a family member, a friend in the Caribbean or in the USA, someone who remembered us and wanted to extend to us a hand of tangible support.

And that, my friend, is the story of how God sustained us through our stay in the Philippines. He who had told us to go went ahead of us to prepare the way and stayed beside us at each step of the journey. Despite one mishap involving Christopher and my occasional illness, our medical bills remained low. Jackie was able to start studying for a Master of Arts in Education, something which we really could not foresee at the beginning. My studies remained right on schedule, allowing me to graduate without unwelcome delays. The children "increased in wisdom and stature" (quoting Luke 2:52), enjoying as much as life at AIIAS could offer and as much as we could afford.

As I indicated earlier, the fat white envelopes stopped coming in January 2006, but by then we had built sufficient reserves to see us through to the end of my studies in March. I had no idea what lay beyond. I had no clue of what I would do after my graduation or how we would pay for the completion of Jackie's studies, but I was able to look back and say that the same God who had brought us thus far would carry us to the end. And He did.

## *Culmination and Call*

January 2006 brought a measure of uncertainty to us. It was my culminating term and just around the corner was my much-anticipated graduation. I got caught up with final assignments and papers and also served on the graduation committee as the class president and song writer. Yet I could not see beyond the gown, the certificate, the hugs and congratulations, the pomp and circumstance of March 3-5.

This sense of insecurity did not sit well with my wife; she needed to have a plan of action. I had kept believing all along that God would open a door of opportunity somewhere, but now it was crunch time. Nerves were beginning to feel the pressure. Something had to happen fast.

As we had done in the past, Jackie and I decided to make this the subject of specific constant prayer. Often we would repair to the prayer garden on the campus, seeking an answer or some guidance from God. I remember that on one occasion the words of this gospel song, written by Phil Johnson, came back to us as we went to pray:

He didn't bring us this far to leave us
He didn't teach us to swim to let us drown
He didn't build His home in us to move away
He didn't lift us up to let us down

The answer came in the form of a notice which had appeared on the AIIAS bulletin board some time in December of 2005. It invited applications to fill a vacant pastoral position in Singapore. At first, when I read it I thought, "Hey, this is not for me. They're asking for someone with a minimum of five years of pastoral experience. I don't have any." So I casually dismissed it. But several weeks later, after some discussion with Jackie, I decided to submit my application. My prayer at that time was "Lord, you know I don't qualify, but if that's what you want for me, then let this application be successful." So we prayed and waited.

Meanwhile, a very tempting prospect also presented itself. Thanks to Mr. Yang's networking, I was offered a teaching position at a newly opened English Language School a short distance away; that would allow me to earn enough money to finance my PhD studies if I so desired. I said it was a tempting opportunity; after all, I could leave AIIAS with a doctoral degree not owing anyone a red cent, as we say back home. I had some time to make up my mind but, not knowing if my application to Singapore would be successful, I decided to take up the teaching offer and agreed to start right after graduation.

The third of March arrived in a blink. In the preceding weeks, I spent much time with the graduating class and sponsor putting together the program and occasionally reviewing and updating our plans. On the musical front, I wrote and taught the class its official song, and I also assembled an international choir to provide the type of music that I felt befitted such a grand occasion. (That certainly reminded me of my days of directing the CUC choir.) Praise God, it all came together quite well and that weekend proved to be one of the most exciting of my life. We were so far from home, but we enjoyed the support of many fellow students, most of whom were members of the African Students Association and the African Choir, which I had started and conducted during the past year.

But soon, as soon as it had arrived, it was all over. The hoods and gowns, the pomp and circumstance, the razzmatazz and "paparazzi," were all gone. By the next day, I was no longer a registered student, which meant that I would have had to vacate the apartment we were renting. Fortunately, my wife was still a student so I was able to remain on her ticket, so to speak. That afforded me the space and time to adjust to my new role in the coming weeks.

So back to teaching I went. For five evenings each week, I would drive to the school in a heavy-looking silver-grey Hyundai Galloper (the Korean version of the Mitsubishi Pajero) which the owners of the school had graciously put in my hands so that I could get to and from the language school hassle free. The sessions were long and most nights I got home between 9:45 and 10:00, but it was fun working with those enthusiastic Korean kids and it gave me much more than what I needed to replace the fat white envelopes which had stopped coming.

Well, early in the month of April, I received word from the president of the Singapore Mission that I had been shortlisted and was therefore invited to attend an interview. The unexpected had happened. I agreed to fly to Singapore that Easter weekend since the language school was also giving everyone a break.

I got to Singapore the Friday night, preached at the prospective church the Sabbath morning, and attended the interview on Sunday morning, returning to AIIAS on Monday. The weekend went quite well: the church was welcoming, the first elder was quite hospitable, and I felt pretty comfortable that I had done a good job with the interview. Yet I was still surprised when, a few days later, the mission president informed me that I had been selected as the new pastor of the Seventh-day Adventist Community Church. What could I say? I had told the Lord that I wanted it to happen ONLY if that was what He had in mind for me at the time; so I felt this was the answer He gave me, and I thanked Him for it.

Graduating from AIIAS, March 2006

The Hyundai Galloper

The feeling of *déjà vu* ("I've seen this before!") hit me when I realized I would have to tell "my boss" at the language school that I was quitting. I remembered having to tell the school board in Bequia something similar. Just as before, I knew they wanted me to stay on longer; how then could I just pull out with a few weeks' notice? But just as before, when I went to speak with the language school's director, who was once a pastor, his reaction put all my fears to rest. He was actually quite pleased at the reason for my imminent departure. To him, this was the Lord's work and he would never do anything to hinder me from responding to the Lord's call. Once more, the problem was solved and I needed not worry.

A fine lesson from the Lord, won't you say? Most certainly. If God wants you to do it, He'll make a way for you to do it. He may leave the obstacles in your path so that you learn to depend on His power, but when He brings you to them you can rest assured that He'll get you over them.

I was due to leave AIIAS on the last day of July to start working in Singapore on the first of August, 2006. Several weeks before my departure, Jackie received a call from the headquarters of the Southern Asia Pacific Division: the Education Director wanted us to drop by his office. At our earliest convenience we did, and there he informed us that the Division was searching for someone to fill the position of Education Director of the Southeast Asia Union Mission whose headquarters is in Singapore, and he thought Jackie was a good candidate. He described at length what the job entailed and invited her to apply.

Now that was a shocker, I must admit. Jackie had not yet completed her studies; she was still in the final stages of writing her thesis, and here came a possible employment opportunity. There we were just a few months earlier, wondering what would become of us after our graduation, and before we knew it, doors were opening to us in a region where we were but "strangers and foreigners."

Again, it sounded too good to be true, but then again, isn't it true that we serve a God of the improbable and the seemingly impossible? Don't we serve a God who has promised to be with us, "even unto the end," a God who promised to finish the good work that he started? He had not just brought us to AIIAS to leave us there; He had other items on His to-do list, and He was not about to quit until He had finished the job.

Glory to His name!

# VII

## IN THE FIELD

> "'You are My servant, I have chosen you and have not cast you away: Fear not, for I am with you; Be not dismayed, for I am your God. I will strengthen you, yes, I will help you, I will uphold you with My righteous right hand.' "Behold, all those who were incensed against you
> Shall be ashamed and disgraced; they shall be as nothing, and those who strive with you shall perish. You shall seek them and not find them—those who contended with you. Those who war against you shall be as nothing, as a nonexistent thing. For I, the Lord your God, will hold your right hand, saying to you, 'Fear not, I will help you.' "Fear not, you worm Jacob, you men of Israel! I will help you," says the Lord and your Redeemer, the Holy One of Israel." Isa 41:8-14

### *Settling in Singapore*

I moved to Singapore on schedule, leaving my family behind for the next three months. Those were difficult days as I struggled to adjust to a new way of life without the support of my family, but we would remain in touch as much as possible via telephone and the internet.

During the second month of my stay, Jackie was called over to Singapore for what turned out to be a successful interview with the Southeast Asia Union Mission. She would serve as Director of Education and Women's Ministries.

There it was: the end of a long period of uncertainty; there is was: the answer to the prayers offered up in the prayer garden. *Voila!* The God in whom we trusted, the God who had taken us through our Red Sea experience, who had filled our financial bucket when it ran dry in early 2004—this same God had seen both of us through, placing us in positions which we never anticipated when we left Bequia: I as a minister with the Singapore Mission, and Jackie as Director of Education and Women's Ministries with the Southeast Asia Union Mission. Who could have told us it would come to this? I can only arrive at one conclusion: God is good!

So on October 27th, at the end of a week of revival preaching, I flew back to AIIAS to help my family prepare to leave what had become their home for the past three years. After a beautiful Sabbath, we spent all of Sunday completing our packing and cleaning the apartment, and on the morning of Tuesday October 31st we all left AIIAS to begin our new life in Singapore.

When we arrived, it was already the end of the academic year for the children, so they had to wait out the long holidays until January when they would be able to start attending the San Yu Adventist School. Jackie decided to spend the next few weeks helping the family adjust to living in Singapore but by the end of November she was on the go. Her departmental responsibilities necessitated her having to do much traveling, for the Union's territory was quite large: Thailand, Cambodia, Laos, Vietnam, Singapore, Peninsular Malaysia, and the two Malaysian states of Sawarak and Saba which are located on the island of Borneo.

The AIIAS experience was now history, but as we settled into a life where things were more visible and where there were set expectations, including an adequate monthly salary, I could not help reflecting ever so often on what it meant to live not by sight but by faith. And as I replayed in my mind the experiences on Bequia, in New York and at AIIAS, the words of two songs often came to mind. The first, by American songwriter Andrae Crouch, contains the lines,

Through it all, through it all,
I've learned to trust in Jesus,
I've learned to trust in God

The second is an old favorite hymn of many Christians. Written by Louisa M.R. Stead in 1882, it reads,

'Tis so sweet to trust in Jesus,
And to take Him at His Word;
Just to rest upon His promise,
And to know, "Thus says the Lord!"

## *Perseverance amid Problems*

For all intents and purposes, the story of my journey to ministry can end here. This was, after all, where I was heading; this is where God was taking me. At least so I thought. But ministry at the Seventh-day Adventist Community Church (SDACC, fondly called *Ez-dak*) proved to be school all over again. I soon discovered that what I had learned at the feet of committed Christian scholars within the seminary walls of AIIAS was not enough; experience was going to be my greatest teacher. And you know what has been said about "Dr. Experience:" he gives the exam first; then he teaches the lesson. That can be pretty painful at times, but God has a way of tempering the pain with seasons of joy and fulfilment.

SDACC was the sort of congregation that you would expect to be strong on the basis of an abundance of talent and skill among its members. There was no shortage of professionals: doctors in the natural and social sciences, successful financiers and seasoned administrators, as well as long-serving denominational workers, just to mention a few. But an ocean of talent and skill does not necessarily result in a strong church. On the contrary, a community whose culture is patterned after Acts 2:42 and 47 will thrive. For it was said of the early church that "they continued steadfastly in the apostles' doctrine and fellowship, in the breaking of bread, and in prayers….And the Lord added to the church daily those who were being saved."

The Southeast Asia Union Headquarters on Thomson Road, Singapore

My family at MacRitchie Reservoir, Singapore, 2006

## THROUGH MIRACLES TO MINISTRY

Those key elements, especially that firm commitment to biblical teaching and to prayer, were not a hallmark of SDACC. The lay leaders were instead more interested in "getting the church right," creating a sense of togetherness so that everyone felt accepted and comfortable. This called for a virtual moratorium on evangelistic activity, the rationale being that one must get one's house in order before seeking to bring new people in. Admittedly, this was a fair line of reasoning; however, my few years of life had taught me that there is never a time when the mission of the church should not be on its front burner. After all, it's our very reason for existence. I had also learned that realistically, the church never gets it right. All one needs to do is read the gospels and the letters of Paul, especially the Corinthian epistles. So I didn't buy into that position.

This difference of perspective accounted significantly but not solely for the lack of momentum that dogged my tenure at SDACC. There were other factors, such as cultural differences and interpersonal conflicts. To begin with, my usually energetic Afro-Caribbean style of preaching, in which I prompted them for "Amens," didn't sit well with some members while others took issue with my occasional singing before or after my sermons. One person was so displeased that within my first three months they sent me a rather unkind anonymous letter reminding me that my role was simply to preach the Bible and not try to show myself as a superstar. What's more, I was operating in a society where challenging or disagreeing with the opinions of the grey-haired men constituted a much greater failure to show respect than my western mentality was aware of, and as a repeat offender in that regard, I unwittingly kept chipping away at the very block on which I was supposed to stand.

As for interpersonal conflicts, they appeared on two fronts. First, it seems that several of the local leaders had long-standing, unresolved differences with the president of the Singapore Mission. As such, they tended to distance themselves and the congregation from whatever program or initiative bore his signature. So from day one, I was caught between a proverbial rock and a hard place. What was I supposed to do: work closely with Administration, or side with the local leaders? It was no easy decision. Second, I realized that certain members in the congregation were being treated with disfavour. I was advised that I would be better off not working with them—even if they were quite willing to work with me. I couldn't have it both ways, if you know what I mean. But how could I take sides and still maintain the integrity of my ministry?

So yes, I spent most of my five years walking a tightrope and managing conflict. We went one step forward and sometimes two steps backward. It was like trying to drive a car whose wheels were stuck in the mud; we were burning up a lot of fuel but getting nowhere. And my characteristically confronting sermons did little to help; they were occasionally the source of much discomfort and the subject of extensive discussion.

But I refused to give up or to roll over and play dead. I repeatedly called the church to seek healing through corporate prayer, and some did respond. Those few willing hearts, usually fewer than ten, joined me as we initiated weekly Wednesday evening study-and-prayer meetings. We studied the entire New Testament and most of the Old; then we launched into a series exploring end-time prophecies using the Amazing Discoveries series called Total Onslaught, presented by South African academic Walter Veith. We also reinstated the annual Week of Prayer and conducted prayers sessions on the first Sabbath of every month, sometimes at breakfast and sometimes on afternoons.

On the evangelistic front, we reached out to the surrounding communities through musical concerts, healthy lifestyle programs in conjunction with Adventist Community Services, literature distribution, and visitation of aged care and special care homes. I also ran two Bible prophecy series to follow up on evangelistic meetings featuring international speaker Mark Finley.

Finally, to bring an extra touch of colour to the Sabbath morning worship experience, I started and directed a choir. Yes, another choir!

But getting back to evangelism: I am from the Caribbean, a region of the world where baptisms routinely number by the scores and hundreds, so it was pretty shocking to come to terms with the low numbers of baptisms among the Adventist congregations in Singapore. I remember praying and asking God to bless us with at least twenty baptisms in the next four years. Now that's pretty conservative from a guy who had seen God perform so many miracles in the preceding years, but I reasoned that given the current situation, an average of five per year would be fantastic. I'm thankful to God that although we did not have twenty baptisms, we came pretty close—seventeen. God be praised!

Why am I talking about this? For two reasons. First, one of the greatest joys of ministry is seeing people give their hearts to Jesus and signify it by going into the waters of baptism. Nothing beats that. Nothing is as heart-warming as seeing the people's eyes light up as the truth of God's word hits them and they respond to Jesus. Second, these baptisms and the joy they brought took place against the odds, against the many challenges that marked my service at SDACC. I therefore saw them as another expression of God's promise, "Fear not, for I am with you; Be not dismayed, for I am your God. I will strengthen you, yes, I will help you, I will uphold you with My righteous right hand." (Isaiah 41:10) They were God's way of telling me that the battle was not mine but His.

There were hard lessons for this pastor to learn and God was not about to spare him. I had always enjoyed the love and favour of others, but I had to learn that being in pastoral ministry is not about enjoying love and favour. Ministry can be tough, bruising, and even hazardous to one's health. It is often beset with criticism, opposition, and sometimes outright rejection. And SDACC was the school of hard knocks, the crucible through which I had to pass in order to slay my misconceptions and resurrect me to a new life of reality.

I also learned that each congregation has its own culture, its own ethos, shaped and informed by decades of history, and that one's success as a pastor depends on his ability to blend in with that culture from the outset. Now I don't think I did well in that regard because in my view, certain aspects of the SDACC culture did not promote church health. So yes, I paid the price.

Finally, I learned that while as a minister I must love everyone, especially those in my care, I cannot afford to trust everyone. True love is unconditional, but trust must be earned and nurtured if it is to be maintained. It's hard to accept sometimes that people who serve and worship with you can shake your hands, walk away, and in the next five minutes, be saying the most unsavory things about you. And guess what: the next time you meet, they're smiling with you like nothing ever happened. But then you find out. Word always gets around. And you ask yourself, "How do I ever trust them again?"

Enough said!

## *Hands of Healing*

Looking back over the years, I have shared with you how God has worked several miracles **for** me. I can never forget those. But I began to feel that it was time for God to work something miraculous **through** me. I think God read my mind, as He alone can, because I never asked Him for such an opportunity but He certainly sent a couple of them my way.

The first was an experience of physical healing. A mother whom I shall not name came to me one day and asked me to come and pray for her daughter, who was suffering from headaches. At first, I began to question whether I was suitable for this task. I wondered whether I had enough faith. But I prayed about it and agreed to go.

When I got to the house, the mother and I agreed to follow the exhortation found in the book of James, chapter five, verses fourteen to fifteen: "Is anyone among you sick? Let him call for the elders of the church, and let them pray over him, anointing him with oil in the name of the Lord. And the prayer of faith will save the sick, and the Lord will raise him up. And if he has committed sins, he will be forgiven." So, agreeing to exercise faith in God's word, we brought out some olive oil; I prayed over it, poured some on the girl's head, and then we both prayed. As we did, I felt a strange new sense of peace sweep over my being. It was as if something... someone had just entered the room and whispered to me, "Erickson, it is done!" I rose from my knees thanking God for what He had accomplished, and I left that apartment smiling as if I had just gotten a million-dollar cash gift.

The next day I called and asked the mother how her daughter was doing.

"Oh, she still has some pain, but it is not as bad as before," she explained.

"Don't worry," I promised; "It's going to be alright."

Sure enough, when I checked a few days later, the headaches had stopped. As far as I know, they have never returned.

The second, an experience of emotional healing, was scarier. I was at church one Wednesday evening awaiting the start of our usual prayer and Bible study session when my mobile phone rang. On the line was another mother whom I knew quite well, a woman who was not part of our church fellowship but who considered me her pastor. She wanted me to come over to her house immediately because her son was very depressed and threatening to end his life.

Nervous and uncertain, I started spinning around while talking to her. I had never dealt with a suicide case before. But here was someone who looked to me for spiritual guidance, someone who needed my help as a pastor. How could I afford to let her down? At the same time, I knew that suicide intervention was something that could be better handled by a professional, someone trained in psychology or counselling.

After a brief discussion with my wife, whose Master's degree had a Counselling Psychology concentration, I caught a cab en route to the house from which the call had come. On the way, I called a member of our church who happened to be a professor of psychology at one of the universities in Singapore and explained my plight to him. He very kindly gave me his professional advice, but after evaluating the situation further, I decided to continue on my way.

Arriving at the house, I found the suicidal young man, whom I had never met before, sitting in the doorway. As I greeted him, he stood up and looked straight into my eyes. That was a look I will never forget: a straight, piercing look that I could have interpreted as "Who told you to come here?" His mum invited me in, thanked me for coming and had us both sit in the living room.

It suddenly dawned on me that this young man wanted someone to listen to him, so I asked him kindly to share his story with me. This he did, going to great lengths to explain his despair. It was a sad story of failure and disappointment, one that understandably pushed him to the brink. I just kept listening, nodding, reflecting, prompting, praying all along; and when he was done, I thanked and affirmed him for being willing to tell me, a total stranger, all about himself.

I still had no idea what I would do next, but I felt impressed to ask him if I could tell him my life story. He agreed, and that's when I began to feel that God had made a breakthrough. So off I went, relating many of the experiences that I've shared in this book to show that while we may have our own plan, God does have His own plan for our lives, one that is ultimately better than anything we may imagine for ourselves. I could see that he was listening with great interest, and by the time I was through with my long story, I thought I would take the chance and ask him whether I could pray for him. To my great delight, he agreed! We knelt together with his mom and dad, who had joined us, and I don't remember what I said, but I could sense from his reaction that something was happening as I was praying. When we got up, I looked to my right and saw a piano, so I felt impressed to ask him whether it was okay if I sang a song.

"Oh, you can play the piano?" he asked, his bright eyes lighting up further.

"Yep," I answered. "Would you mind?"

"Go ahead," he urged, by now sounding quite a different person from the one who started telling me his story about an hour earlier.

So I went to the piano and played and sang the first tune that came to my head—something about serving Jesus every day of my life if I could do it again. When I was done, he was smiling, as was his mother. It was as if a light had been switched on in his soul. After a few more minutes of soaking in the relief, his parents thanked me for coming and called a cab to take me back home.

I left that house that evening with a profound sense of joy in my heart, knowing that God had used me to intervene in someone's life and to give him a renewed sense of hope. The young man turned a corner that night. He got his life back together and moved on, and the last time I checked, he was still alive!

## *Fulfilling the Foretold:*

Toward the end of 2009, the church leaders in Singapore advised me that they were considering me for ordination. (That's when someone is officially set aside for pastoral ministry through a special ceremony that involves other ministers laying hands on him and praying for him.) The news came as a surprise to me but I said, "Lord, that's your business. I didn't ask for it, so it's all up to you."

After several weeks and a few sessions of counselling and interviews, the ordination ceremony took place at the Balestier Road Seventh-day Adventist Church on the afternoon of Saturday February 27, 2010. Two other pastors were ordained at the same time.

As I sat there with Jackie beside me, I couldn't help but reflect on the long road we had travelled. I also remembered one pastor, Samuel Telemacque from Dominica, prophesying in 2002 that I would be ordained in 2010 and that I would one day preach in the Solomon Islands, Fiji, and Papua New Guinea. At least the first part of his prophecy was right on target; the rest was up to God. But for now, what mattered was the joy of being officially recognized by the church leadership as one who had been called by God.

Ordination day, February 27, 2010

Admittedly it was not all joy. It was also a moment of sober reflection. I thought about my parents and my siblings who were so far away and who, therefore, could not be there to share the experience. I also thought of how long we might be in Singapore and what lay beyond that stint—what was next on God's agenda for us. And as I reflected, I found assurance in the words of this hymn, written in 1875 by Fanny Crossby:

All the way my Savior leads me,
What have I to ask beside?
Can I doubt His tender mercy,
Who through life has been my Guide?

## *Pathway to Perth*

By April of 2010, my wife and I began to sense that it was time to move on. Chilling winds of change were beginning to blow at our workplaces. Not only were the signs becoming clearer to us, but friends who were concerned about our wellbeing also began to suggest that we should seriously consider bringing the curtain down on our ministry and service in Singapore.

But what would such a move entail? And where would it take us? We had absolutely no idea. We considered a few options, including returning to the Philippines so that Jackie could pursue a PhD, but we didn't want to run ahead of God. Just like we'd done in the past, we wanted to be sure that we were following His directions, not our own hunches.

So we decided, as before, to make this a matter of focused prayer. We prayed continually and specifically for God's guidance for the next six months… yes, six months, before one door opened up.

Around September of that year, I became aware of a great need for pastors in the Persian Gulf region so I submitted an expression of interest. I must confess that in spite of doing so, I had strong, lingering doubts. I was not sure how my family, especially my wife and daughter, would adapt to living in that part of the world, given the strict Islamic culture there. I just had to be absolutely sure that this was the correct decision. So even while I kept communicating with the leadership in that region, I kept consulting my Leader, the same one who had led me "all the way."

Things came down to the wire, so to speak. I received confirmation from Administration in the Gulf Region that they had voted to assign me to the Abu Dhabi and Al-Ain congregations and they were simply waiting for final word on my availability to commence service in January 2011. But the very next week, I received a call from Pastor Glen Townend, then President of the Western Australian Conference asking me if I would consider relocating to Perth to serve as Pastor of the Livingston Church.

So now, after months and weeks of waiting, I suddenly had two options on the table.

But wait! Isn't it amazing how God does His thing sometimes? You pray and pray and pray; He keeps you waiting and waiting and waiting. And then He just drops it on you! Instead of one, you end up with two or more—"good measure, pressed down, shaken together, and running over" (Luke 6:38). Isn't it true that sometimes we receive little because we ask for little?

Back to my two options on the table: As I thought about them over the next few days, it was clear that the Australian one would answer all my questions relating to the welfare of my family. So without much delay, I accepted the call to Perth. The rest, as they say, is history.

Arriving in Perth, June 26, 2011

## *Final Faith-notes*

Now, in my eighth year of pastoral ministry, I remain ever grateful to God for leading me along this incredible journey, through many miraculous events, to this point. I think about the fact that I am now serving His people in as far a place as Australia (in relation to the Caribbean, of course) and acknowledge that this couldn't have happened without Him. I also remain ever committed to fulfilling the design He had in mind while He kept calling me through all those years.

"I love to tell the story" of God's amazing goodness, of how He guides and provides, of how He is able to do for us much more than we can ever imagine. I've seen so many people encouraged and inspired by it that I can't shut up.

I realize that so many believers today "tremble on the brink" when their faith is tested that it almost looks normal, but I'd like to look them in the face and say, "Hey, hold on. Don't let go. Trust God. It doesn't matter what kind of challenge you are facing or how formidable it seems. If you would just exercise some unrelenting, unyielding, rock-solid faith in a God who was, who is, and who always will be greater than our every challenge, He would do amazing things for you. After all, He is still the God of miracles.

Maybe you think that God has called or is still calling you to some specific line of service for Him; maybe you're not one hundred per cent sure that what you're sensing is indeed His call. Maybe you're hearing noises like Samuel did, but you're not sure who's speaking. Just ask Him. Ask Him to show you clearly. Ask, like Saul (Paul) did on the Damascus Road, "Lord, what do You want me to do?" (Acts 9:6). Ask persistently. Ask earnestly. Ask in faith without wavering. Just ask! For never has such a question been asked that God did not answer.

You might think that you are weak in faith, but guess what: God's grace is sufficient for you and His strength is made perfect in your weakness (see 2 Corinthians 12:9). And rest assured that when you move forward in obedience to His word, He will be with you at every step. He has strewn your path with promises that cannot fail. He will part the waters for you. No mountain will block your way. He will wet the fleece or keep it dry, if He chooses, just to confirm His word. After all, He is still the God of miracles.

Maybe you've already answered the call and you're at college or university, struggling with limited finances or academic overload, or both. Remember that you serve a God of the seemingly impossible. Go back to the Sea of Galilee. See Him walking there, calling fishermen to be fishers of men and demonstrating His power through a miraculous catch of fish. He is more than able to fill your net. He who ordered the ravens to bring bread to His servant Elijah, and later commanded a nameless widow in a foreign country to take care of him—this same God will make adequate arrangements to meet your needs. Don't worry about how He's going to do it; that is HIS business. Just trust Him. After all, He is still the God of miracles.

Finally, maybe you're already out there in the field and you're having a hard time. Taking care of the Lord's sheep can sometimes be quite rough. Sometimes it's even dangerous, because they are not all sheep who look like sheep. Wolves there may be among your flock. You may be challenging the schemes of politicians, dodging the bullets of snipers, or contending with the fallacies of heretics. You're stressed. In fact, you've just about had it. You are seriously contemplating quitting. Like Elijah, you're crying, "It is enough! Now, Lord, take my life!" (1 Kings 19:4).

If that's your case, I've got a little message for you, and it comes from 1 Samuel 30:6: "Now David was greatly distressed, for the people spoke of stoning him, because the soul of all the people was grieved, every man for his sons and his daughters. But David strengthened himself in the Lord his God." There it is: encourage yourself in the Lord your God, for He who called you is the ever-faithful, unchanging God. God has not given you "a spirit of fear, but of power and of love and of a sound mind" (2 Timothy 1:7). Ministry may be tough, but God is tougher still. So hang tough. Don't quit. Trust God. After all, He is still the God of miracles.

# VIII

## Epilogue

Let me introduce you to a very good friend of mine. She's sharp, sensitive, and super smart. What makes her so smart? It's simple: her vision! She's got the best pair of eyes, the ideal, perfect, 20/20 vision.

Her name? Hindsight!

I have a love-hate relationship with Hindsight. I like the fact that she helps me "understand it better by and by." I love it when she sneaks up behind me as I'm sitting there, sorting and sifting through sequences of events, trying to make sense of it all, and she just gently and quietly rests her hand on my shoulder and, smiling, whispers, "Look back." I love the way she brings me around to those "Aha!" moments where gratitude kisses disbelief, where I realise that despite my blindness I did make the right decision—thank God! But I always find myself wishing that contrary to her nature, she would come to my rescue in the present, NOT in the future when the moment of decision has long passed.

Hindsight: she's a gem, a really good friend.

But lest we end up giving Hindsight all the credit, let me set the record straight: she is only as good as time permits. What's more, she thrives on the amazing patience of a merciful and gracious God who not only holds time in His hands but is also uniquely gifted with hindsight, insight and foresight; a God who relentlessly pursues the objects of His love. So even as I am tempted to sing, in the words of Johnny Nash, "I can see clearly now, the rain has gone," I am reminded that it has only eventuated because God never gave up on me. He never quit calling and waiting. He just stuck with me.

Isn't He wonderful? Don't just sit there reading. Go ahead and praise Him!

*Points to Ponder—Six More:*

Let's return to my observations about the divine call, continuing from Chapter One where we affirmed that God's call often comes in the context of miracles. Here's what, with the blessing of Hindsight, I've come up with.

*Number Two: God can change or add to the task to which He calls someone.*

The call is God's divine prerogative. He is sovereign; He is in charge, and without any human input whatsoever, He calls whomever He wishes to do whatever He wishes.

I've said it before: God doesn't get stuck in a rut the way we humans are prone to do. Our thinking is so limited! We're often so one-tracked, and it's such a mistake to project that thinking onto God. We reason—misguidedly—that if God has called someone named Mike to go fish, that's all that God wants Mike to do for the rest of his life.

Not necessarily so!

In our introductory story, Luke records that "Jesus said to Simon, 'Do not be afraid. From now on you will catch men'" (Luke 5:10). But later, the Master had a few different words for his impetuous disciple: "Simon, Simon! Indeed, Satan has asked for you, that he may sift you as wheat. But I have prayed for you, that your faith should not fail; and when you have returned to Me, strengthen your brethren" (Luke 22:31-32).

What? Build up the church, sort of? That doesn't sound like fishing; that's more like looking after the tank of fish!

Hold on; there's more. John recounts that following His resurrection, Jesus gave Peter an additional job description: "Feed my sheep; ...feed my lambs" (John 21:15-17). There you go: Peter is now a shepherd! It doesn't tell us he is no longer a fisherman, but he definitely has a new responsibility—feeding the sheep.

You know what that tells me? It says that I may be a pastor or an evangelist today but somewhere down the road, God in His wisdom may call me to serve as a consultant or as an ambassador. We are therefore mistaken when we draw a box of human parameters around the divine call by saying that because God does not change, He cannot call someone from one line of service to another. Remember, the call is His initiative and the choice of task is His prerogative, not ours.

*Number Three: God repeatedly calls unsuspecting men and women.*

We read of seers and deliverers, prophets and prophetesses, kings and queens, disciples and apostles, who were simply caught off guard by the call. As far as I know, none of those chosen ones saw it coming. Not a single one of them was sitting there saying, "Hey, I'm waiting for God to call me. I just love the idea of being called, so I'm going to position myself to be right in line for that call." No! It's always been a case where God, whose omniscient gaze goes far deeper than outward appearance, looks into the heart of that person and sees, not a fisherman, not a shepherd boy, not a brilliant law graduate, but a "chosen vessel." It's always a case where the ones being called are often caught by surprise. It's the last thing on their minds.

Here's a case in point: Saul, the first king of Israel. We find him one day at the end of a long, hot, fatiguing, frustrating, eventually-futile mission to find his father's lost donkeys. That's it! He's got nothing else up his sleeve. In fact, he has practically given up the search. He just wants to go home, kick off his dusty sandals, and flop down into his favourite couch. But at the urging of his servant, he decides to make a stop at the seer's home peradventure the man of God can tell him where those asses can be found.

## THROUGH MIRACLES TO MINISTRY

So up to the door he walks. And out comes Samuel, who, on greeting him, seizes his hand firmly and gives him a hard, piercing look as if to remind Saul of his credentials:

"I am the seer!"

"Go up ahead of me to the high place," Samuel continues, "for today you are to eat with me, and in the morning I will send you on your way and will tell you all that is in your heart. As for the donkeys you lost three days ago, do not worry about them; they have been found. And to whom is all the desire of Israel turned, if not to you and your whole family line?" (1Samuel 9:19-20, NIV)

Saul is flabbergasted! I can almost hear him stammer, "What? Wha'...what? No-no-no! Why are you talking to me like this? You don't understand. I belong to the tribe of Benjamin, the smallest tribe in Israel, and my family is the least important one in the tribe. No; you've got the wrong man, Samuel. I couldn't... Uh... I can't! Period. I'm not even good at finding asses! So... forget it!" Saul obviously doesn't think he is worthy of the call.

Which brings me to my fourth point—

*Number Four: God's call has a better success rate with people who sense their unworthiness.*

It seems to work best with those who know that their characters need a complete makeover, people whose résumés make for horrible reading, people whose sense of self-worth finds its best expression in the words of the prophet Isaiah: "Woe to me!" I cried. "I am ruined! For I am a man of unclean lips, and I live among a people of unclean lips" (Isaiah 6:5, NIV). Moses saw himself as a terrible speaker (Exodus 4:10). Jeremiah protested, "Almighty LORD, I do not know how to speak. I am only a boy" (Jeremiah 1:6, GW)! Gideon was threshing wheat under cover, hiding from the Midianites (Judges 6:11). Amos knew that he was neither a prophet nor the son of a prophet, just a mere herdsman and a gatherer of sycamore fruit (Amos 7:14). And Peter, in our opening story, could only cry out, "Depart from me; for I am a sinful man, O Lord" (Luke 5:8). Indeed, God cannot do much with people who are great in their own eyes; He takes the lowly in heart and the contrite in spirit.

*Number Five: God's call is never an afterthought.*

Never! Never ever! Whenever He calls, it's because He has gotten to the point in His calendar where He is ready to enact the very plan He had drawn up even before the one being called was conceived. Ask the prophet Jeremiah; he'll tell you clearly in verses 4 and 5 of the first chapter of the book that bears his name. "The word of the LORD came to me, saying, 'Before I formed you in the womb I knew you, before you were born I set you apart; I appointed you as a prophet to the nations."

Now this guarantees that whether we sense it or not, God remains fully aware of every incline or descent, every rock, tree stump, or pothole in the road along which He calls His servant to travel. God said of the newly-converted Saul of Tarsus, "This man is my chosen instrument to carry my name before the Gentiles and their kings and before the people of Israel; I will show him how much he must suffer for my name" (Acts 9:15-16, NIV). And true to this declaration, the apostle endured arrests, court trials, beatings, stoning, imprisonment, abandonment, and shipwreck, only to be executed at the end. He really suffered. But God was watching. More than that, God was guiding His life.

I think that it's very important for people who have been called to recognize this truth. It can help to keep their faith firmly fastened when they face overwhelming and unfavourable circumstances, in the midst of which they are tempted to feel they were not called after all or that the One who called them has somehow abandoned them to fend for themselves. Hey, God does not just show up when things get tough. God does not simply come running to catch up; God is already there, not just in the present but in the future. Just like he sent an angel to reassure Paul that there would be no loss of life in the imminent shipwreck (Acts 27:23), he will send His word to reassure you, dear reader, that He remains very proactively in charge.

*Number Six: God's call is persistent.*

He calls, not once, nor twice, but several times over, especially when His call is not perceived the first, second, or even the third time. I think of Samuel: the lad thought he was hearing Eli's aging voice, only to learn after the third experience that it was actually the voice of God. Sometimes God gives his servant extra time to gain some much-needed strength for the journey ahead. This was true of Elijah who, fleeing for his life from the face of Jezebel, ended up among the rocks of Horeb—the same mountain where Moses had encountered the Lord at the burning bush. God came to Elijah twice with the same call: "What are you doing here, Elijah?" (1Kings 19:9,13). Here, again, we see displayed the persistence, incomparable patience, and faithfulness of God. For this, we ought to be truly thankful. After all, it is only because of these attributes that many of God's servants today, myself included, got a second and third opportunity, the blessings of which we now enjoy.

*And finally, Number Seven: God does not call everyone to carry out the same specific task.*

Sometimes we forget that. Sometimes we begin questioning, like Peter did down at the beach after Christ's resurrection, "Lord, what about this man?" We need to remember Jesus' reply: "If I will that he remain till I come, what is that to you? You follow Me" (see John 21:20-22). It's like, "Hey, if I want him to wait until I return, then that would be my wish for him. Don't worry about him. Just concentrate on what I've asked you to do. Got it?"

In one sense, God's purpose is the same for everyone: He wants us to build His kingdom. But that kingdom has so many facets that we cannot all be teachers, preachers or healers. God calls some to be administrators, others to be accountants, and still others to be keepers of the church's property. Again, our part is not to sit and rue our lot, reasoning that we might have been better off had we been accorded another responsibility—one far more glorious in our eyes—like the one with which such and such a brother or sister has been blessed. Our duty, instead, is to take His yoke upon ourselves and learn from Him (see Mathew 28:29) how we might carry that yoke in a manner that glorifies Him.

Last words—just two: Trust God!

Printed in Australia
AUOC02n1655270115
265477AU00002B/2/P